SWEDISH MASSAGE

SWEDISH MASSAGE

A systematic and practical approach

by

John F. Harris, MSF

L. N. Fowler & Co. Ltd.
1201/3 High Road
Chadwell Heath
Romford Essex RM6 4DH

ISBN 0 85243 369 7

Printed and bound at
The Camelot Press Ltd, Southampton

In Memory of

FRANCES FINUCANE, my great grandmother,
and
JACQUELINE SONIA, my wife,

who, in their different ways
instilled in me a deep respect
for nature and human contact

Contents

Illustrations

Foreword

by

Ian A. Scott, OBE, ND, DO

Whether used therapeutically or as a means of bringing relaxation and a sense of well-being, massage is one of the earliest therapies known to mankind and perhaps the most universal. In Egypt, Greece and Rome, the centres of civilization, the talented masseur was as essential a member of society as the physician and as highly respected. Using nothing but his hands and his little stocks of aromatic oils, he brought comfort to those racked with pain, release from stress to the over-wrought and renewed vigour to the exhausted.

Massage is an art and even with all the techniques not everyone can be a master of this art. To excel one must have an intuitive sense of touch and hands with a confidence and instinct of their own; when this is so the masseur becomes an agent for healing. Without this intuition, but with an understanding of the techniques, benefit is still considerable though at a somewhat lower level. Today, as in other fields, only a few are talented masseurs the rest being good, bad or indifferent.

As a former Principal of two of the largest 'health hydros' in England, where massage plays an important part in the therapies practised, I have had much experience at the 'receiving end' of the hands of many masseurs and I have no hesitation in classing John Harris as one with the hands and intuition of a master of the art, as his many students can testify, and this little book sets out clearly and in easily-understood stages, the movements and techniques forming the basis of the art of massage. No book can do more and there are few available which do as much. Students wishing to become masseurs are advised to read it carefully and practise the techniques assiduously; if they do, many will become proficient and some may actually achieve mastery of an important branch of the healing arts.

Preface

During my travels I have noticed that books which both lucidly explain and illustrate the art of Swedish Massage are in short supply. By saying this I am not suggesting that there is an inadequate number of health books on the general market. Not in the least; however, I have noticed that the accent in most instances is on methods of eastern influence. In this book I hope to present to the reader a formula by which he may safely work, the system: 'Swedish Massage'. I would like you to realise that this is only the aperitif. The following pages are a guide to help you, an introduction that you may follow. Here is a system that can, with practice and effort, become the realization of a most venerable art. If you treat massage with the respect that it deserves, it will respond to its advocates with favour; an 'extra-communication'.

For those of you who wish to become more deeply involved, further theoretical as well as practical tuition will be necessary. In this book, whenever possible, the vernacular as well as the correct medical term has been used. I would like to suggest that prior to your practical exercises you read the appropriate section; then you may proceed to that area of the body. Concentrate upon this region for approximately a week, or indeed longer; this really is necessary for you to develop a good technique and understanding. Then, and only then, proceed to the next section. The views given in this book are in most cases my own, arising from my experience over a number of years in England as well as in other countries.

I would like to thank those who have helped me in preparing this manuscript, particularly the late Ian A. Scott, O.B.E., N.D., D.O., for proofing the medical text and writing the foreword. To Mike Adkins and Anne, for initial proofing of the literary content. To Roy Clements, for ideas and suggestions. To Jennie Lamb and Sally Bell, for posing as models. The photographers: David Nicholls of Worthing for producing most of the photographs, Les Fuller of Worthing for figure numbers 2B and 12A, and a friend who wishes to remain anonymous.

Worthing 1982

Introduction

Massage is the applied art of manipulating the soft tissues of the body. Swedish massage is a defined system following the teaching of Pehr Henrik Ling, a Swede from Stockholm, recognized for his objective approach towards physical culture. Massage is to be recommended as a prophylactic, because with it, we can raise the health of the healthy and as a healing agent it can be beneficially applied in the treatment of certain functional disorders. Our art is supremely capable of treating the indisposed as well as the fit.

Evidently, you have already taken the first step towards giving and receiving massage. To enjoy the exercises without rushing and to arrange as much practice as possible would be an excellent idea. Massage has been practised in every age and on every continent; it has stood the test of time. Those who excel in this art will most certainly be much sought after.

A short note on contributory aids to health. Health-farms with their fresh garden produce, as well as systems of dieting, can only be good. There is, however, a snag: it is an expensive way to discipline oneself. In these establishments you may exercise, eat vegetarian insecticide-free products, quenching your thirst with lemon water. Fortunately, people are becoming conscious of the quality and quantity of the food they eat. To be aware of such things suggests a healthy mental attitude towards the body. Half the world seeks ways of getting rid of unwanted fat, fat that is indeed killing them; the other half seek food in order that they may live. It would be to our ultimate benefit if we could find a balance before it is too late.

Turkish baths with their soap-applying-attendants, are now a commodity of a past age. They have been replaced by saunas from Finland which are extremely popular. We are becoming aware of our physical body and its needs.

The dedicated masseur, in spite of countless advertisements in local journals, regrettably is hard to find. Allow me to assure you that he does exist. Now I invite you to read on and enjoy your new found tactile dimension.

History and Myth

From the earliest of writings, rubbing has been used as a healing agent. Kong-Fu in his books of approximately 3000 BC, mentions massage. The Chinese and the Japanese of today rate massage highly in their therapies. Massage is also mentioned among the sacred books of the Hindus. The practice of massage was highly developed and extensively used by the ancient Greeks, Romans and Egyptians. Homer, 1000 BC, refers in his 'Odyssey' to beautiful women rubbing and anointing war-worn heroes to refresh them. Hypocrates, 380 BC, comments on massage in depth. He used the Greek term 'Anatripsis', which means rubbing up.

Celsus, a Roman physician of early Christian times, advocated the use of daily frictions in the sun. He also stated that paralysed limbs can be strengthened by being rubbed. Julius Cæsar, 55 BC, received frictions to alleviate the neuralgic pains from which he suffered.

During the middle ages massage fell into disuse, at least in Europe, until a physician and surgeon, Ambrose Pare, resurrected it in 1580. In 1813 at Stockholm, the Royal Central Institute was established, and Pehr Henric Ling taught his system of scientifically arranged movements. Ling was to massage and physiotherapy, what Segovia was to the Spanish Guitar. In fact hospitals often included a massage department until the early 1900s.

If the personal contribution of hand massage was ever neglected, then society in general would be the poorer. Although sophisticated apparatus has ingeniously complemented human effort, these instruments could never replace it.

There are other aspects of massage dealing with beauty, which, non-therapeutic, have a place in society today.

Hygiene and the Clothes You Wear

Short sleeves are to be recommended for all occasions. An overall, a plain thin plastic apron, a smock; a dentist's or an osteopath's jacket can be ideal. Cotton will keep you cooler than man-made fabrics. Do not overdress, as you will need ventilation. Heat generates more heat and causes considerable discomfort. It is indeed sensible to wear casual shoes or sandals. Whatever you wear, your appearance is of utmost importance. White should always be white, never grey. What you look like is how you will be remembered.

Your approach to hygiene is not only personal, but essential. You will, I feel sure, fully understand the implications of washing ones hands before as well as after each massage treatment. A change of towel or serviette, on a one-for-each-client basis, is not only desirable but imperative. Finally clean, short, well kept finger nails and hands, are the tools for the job; treat them well.

In further pages, reference will be made to the 'client' when speaking of the person being massaged. This is not entirely correct, as it necessarily conjures up scenes of payments being given for services rendered. However, for the purpose of this book let us accept that the recipient of the massage shall be the 'client'.

The Treatment Room

The room in which you receive clients, should be light and with adequate ventilation. A vase of flowers or a leaf plant can be pleasing to the eye. The window should be sufficiently curtained, or ideally have a Venetian blind. Remember that the smaller the room, the easier it will be to keep warm during the winter months. Your specific work bench is referred to either as a couch, a plinth or sometimes a table, the ideal height of your table being somewhere in the region of 28 to 30 inches, depending on your own particular height and preference. A good guide is to stand against the table with your arm extended in a downward direction; bend your hand at right angles so that the flat of the hand lies a few inches above the surface. This usually is considered a practical height at which to work. Do remember that your back will be under stress whilst giving the massage and as the treatment is likely to last about 45 minutes, it is advisable to get everything correct first. Should your couch prove to be too low for you, a carpenter can make wooden blocks with recesses for holding the legs, thereby raising the couch one or two inches. Massage plinths are becoming an expensive item to buy, particularly if they are portable. However, with a little ingenuity it is possible to make one's own. For those of you who wish to purchase a couch, some addresses are given at the end of this book in the Appendix. It is well to bear in mind that one can always improvise. I have used lounge tables of the correct height, however, I must emphatically advise one and all against giving massage on a bed; unless of course your client is a genuine patient! Unfortunately beds are usually too low, wide and soft.

The plinth is draped with a sheet or a large towel, also a thin pillow is a refinement to give support to the head. This could prove easy to make perhaps by using a thin piece of plastic foam. An ordinary pillow is much too thick and bends the cervical vertebrae in the neck, resulting in bad posture. A roll of foam or a pillow should be kept handy to place under your client's knees. This raises the legs and relaxes the abdomen when applying massage to that area. A screen or curtained recess at the end of the room, behind which the client may undress, is an excellent idea. A bath-robe here would be very useful, or a large towel if you prefer. Although not essential it is professional practice and shows consideration to have a well appointed room.

What to Use: Powder, Creams, Oils or Alcohol?

Since the beginning of time, countless different agents have been employed as a medium for massage. Herbs, creams, powders; oils, animal and vegetable fats, have all been used. It is what you the masseur or masseuse can work with best which will determine your choice. These applications possess certain virtues and in some cases vices.

The following is a general guide only, and by no means exhaustive. Allow me to invite you into the labyrinth of preparations, remembering that whatever you decide to use is only to allow the free movement of your hands over the body.

POWDER

Powder is a worthy standby for situations in which an invalid, although bedridden, could benefit from a localised massage. Since powder, unlike oils, will not stain or stick to clothes or sheets, the person confined can rest immediately after the treatment without having to change position.

A rest is always indicated after a full-body massage. It aids recovery and the practice of resting a client, whether healthy or ill, should always be observed. A little thought will readily suggest that any abrupt muscular strain or bending should be avoided by a sick person who has spent some time immobile. Therefore, if no immediate wash is necessary, full remedial-action is allowed to register.

Such vital benefits are expected to follow a massage treatment because depth-effect is a consequence of this art. We render a person malleable, encouraging nature to heal; what could be more natural?

CREAMS

Creams are compounded from a wide range of animal and vegetable by-products. Flowers, roots, herbs – gathered from the exotic orient or from our home-gardens and variably mixed with lanolin, wax, or oil of almonds – all play an important cosmetic part in the preparation of cream. Further to this, discerning members of this science have paid tribute to nature in their inclusion of the essence Rose and Jasmin as well as other plants. The world of cosmetology is full of ancient and modern recipes. If you like the idea of experimenting and concocting your own preparations, then it is within your grasp to do so. There are quite a number of works in the reference section of public libraries awaiting your perusal. These suggest, as well as instruct, on how you may make a number of different potions in your home.

Catherine de Medici, after having consulted her physician, is reputed to have picked early morning dew-drenched peach-blossoms, to have crushed them with the oil of almonds, and to have accomplished this feat by the light of the moon. Do not laugh too loudly; the mystique of a past age still remains very much with us. As you know, one's belief in something, allows one to become its beneficiary. Add to this, a romantic and acceptable authority and life itself responds to its finely-blended mysteries.

Creams are to be especially recommended for neck and facial massage, as nothing is more suitable for this area. There are other uses; here are suggestions as to where benefit would certainly ensue from application of a salve: in cases where one's client has an allergy to oil, when a person is bedridden, for localized areas of the body, and when evening clothes are to be donned immediately afterwards.

For general massage I rarely use cream as I find it has a tendency to be absorbed far too quickly, although I know of a health farm that only uses cream for its massage treatments. A sensible approach therefore, would be to have a jar of cream; it is a useful adjunct, this depending of course on your own preference and your clients needs.

Almond oil is most excellent. It was used in Imperial Rome as well as in mediæval Europe. Even today, cosmetic manufacturers use it as a base in many of their preparations. To use this oil in general massage is an expensive practice; however, should you have a supply, do use it.

Olive oil is a superior oil to use in most cases where there is scar tissue. The thick viscosity of this oil is soothing and protects damaged skin. Wheatgerm oil is also excellent for post operational scars, as it has a high vitamin E content which is renowned for aiding healing processes. Naturally, an intuitive touch is also necessary to prevent distress.

Safflower oil is a very fine oil; moderately priced and obtainable from most health food shops and some supermarket stores. It can be recommended to all for general use without fear of contradiction. Its content is good, its hand-to-body relationship excellent; so use this oil for any body treatment. I am using safflower oil at the present moment. It certainly has the right viscosity.

Sunflower-seed oil is another good oil that you may use, however, it is unfortunate that it has the disadvantage of staining towels and other fabrics yellow.

Mustard-seed oil is a localized oil found in abundance in India, and used extensively by the natives of that country. Availability seems to dictate what one uses.

Coconut oil from the West Indies may be tempting. It is an exceedingly good oil but in its natural form the aroma of unrefined coconut can be most pronounced. Nevertheless, when bought in this country it is usually refined. During cold weather it may solidify and consequently it will be necessary to liquefy before use by placing your oil bottle for a few minutes in warm water. This is a good idea for any oil during cold weather; before applying the oil to your client's body, warm it, as well as your hands first.

The above are some examples of vegetable oils and being extracted from living vegetation they are liable to become rancid. This is often the case when they are kept for too long or stored in a warm place. It is recommended that you keep your oil in a cool cupboard or storage place, not however, in a refrigerator. It is also an advantage to buy small quantities of oils rather than maintaining large reserves. A half to one litre should be plenty for most people. There are also mineral oils, many baby oils coming into this category.

In some instances they are produced from petroleum by-products. Mothers tend to like this oil as it is usually 'easy' on their babies' clothes, because it does not stain. As far as massage is concerned, my advice is to find and use a pure natural product whenever possible. Experiment until you find an oil that you are happy to work with. I advise you against the use of aromatic oils or scents; one of your client's may like what is not acceptable to another. Using aromatic oils can be quite interesting, but neutral is playing it safe, unless you happen to be an aromatherapist.

In following my advice and suggestions on what you may use, you will probably notice that the viscosity of any individual oil varies. Usually this is more noticeable when an oil is purchased in a supermarket and compared with another from a natural-food shop. For the purpose of massage, a heat-extracted oil is usually thinner, less expensive and more suitable for general use. As there is no exact guide, you will need to try out various extracts, bearing in mind what has already been said.

ALCOHOL

Alcohol is a spirit. It is highly combustible and can burn the eyes as well as other delicate membranes of the body, so should you be tempted to use it, do pay particular attention to where it is applied. There are many types of alcohol: the sort one drinks obviously cannot be used for what we have in mind. Surgical spirit is not very good either because of an additive making it unpleasant to use and to smell. Isopropynol is quite good, but apart from being expensive, is too severe: it removes the oil too quickly and is harsh on the skin. My own preference is a spirit called Ethanol, an industrial methylated spirit.

To obtain pure alcohol, a chemist will require signed, dated authority from you before he can issue it. This in the first instance will have to be obtained from H.M. Customs; each application for authority to buy will be considered individually. The Customs will want to know exactly how you propose using it, e.g. for eliminating excessive oil from the body (especially should the client be incapacitated), to sterilise the hands, to stimulate the client's back prior to using tapotement, and during hot weather. You will be required to keep the spirit in a padlocked metal cupboard. This whole procedure might be considered a lot of trouble since the use of spirits is not an essential.

Study; Approach; Attunement; Art

This art of our choice reaches a high degree of effectiveness when we add new thought to familiar knowledge. Ethically, each person who entrusts himself to our understanding, as well as our ability to alleviate from tension and certain pathological conditions, is to be given of our best. To approach every situation with concentrated awareness of, and absolute confidence in our ability, is to honour that mutual trust.

Study of data is, of course, fundamental; when this is put into practice it becomes meaningful. Facts relate to us when their reality is within our experience. Whilst living in a body of our own, each of us takes tuition so as to evaluate it. Thus intuition is necessary for our own fulfilment and for meeting a client's needs.

Attunement, to a person's state of mind and level of relaxation, may appear to some as routine in its challenge, while to others, too high a goal to reach. However, deep relaxation is a phenomenon of peace and calm; which assuming that one is receiving treatment, will only occur through mutual recognition. You will appreciate that to relax to a degree where empathy ensues, could result in the absolute establishment of thought and touch communication.

All of us realize that the practice of an art is a joy, and that any discipline which is practised without joy, is robbed of its art status. Thus it is very necessary to enjoy massage with its implied commitment and reverence for the mind and body. If personal empathy should ever prove to be impossible, then you have the choice of practising with expertise alone, or of declining to proceed. You will probably agree that referring your client to another practitioner at this point is mutually acceptable, for the practical reasons of suitability, speciality, or success rate. With this art you can never reach the ultimate, perfection being limitless.

Adjustable Hands and Classical Physiological Findings

We are now obliged to leave the abstract and spiritual implications of the previous chapter, returning to the harsh world of facts. If you can link facts with high ideals, then you will indeed be travelling in the right direction. Success is when you inwardly feel a surge of knowledge; when you KNOW that you have indeed succeeded. This could be where healing of a higher nature takes over, but that is a subject of depth that we cannot go into here. By keeping the ideal pure, the action justifies itself: nonetheless, there are rules and cautions, which you will appreciate as you progress.

During massage the metabolism of the body is increased. Laboratory-tested blood counts, taken before and immediately after a deep massage, have revealed an increase of red corpuscles in the blood of up to 25%; on occasion even higher. The urine output is notably increased. Blood pressure is considerably lowered as a direct result of general massage. I feel sure that no one would fail to appreciate the significance of this. The nerves, as well as all living cells, are stimulated, generally causing a condition of tone in the area being treated. Lymph as well as venous return, is assisted on its journey back to the heart. Friction can start a peristaltic action when applied to the colon direct; thereby clearing away congested body waste and toxins. Ultimately tension is broken down, allowing the body being treated to function and recognize itself again.

Massage for the Fit and Indisposed

Indications for massage:– in the first place virtually anyone can have and benefit from massage, nevertheless there are some exceptions which we shall discuss in the following paragraphs. Naturally, common sense must be paramount in all judgments relating to a person's physical condition. Think clearly and when in doubt, don't. Now let us return to the positive side and state that a person in good health, can benefit further by having general massage. By 'general', the whole of the body is indicated.

You may in all probability be asked to give massage to a pregnant lady. In such a case, it is generally considered safe to massage up to three months or thereabouts, although it would be wise to avoid any contact with the abdomen and lower back area. If the pregnancy is more advanced and without complications, it is still safe to give a GENTLE, LIMITED, MASSAGE to the extremities, e.g. the arms, legs and the neck ONLY would benefit considerably from a careful treatment. Always remember that gentleness is a prerequisite for any expectant mother or aged person.

Should a person with a fractured limb require massage, you may give massage to the rest of the body carefully avoiding the limb in question. In cases of swelling or severe bruising, you may massage the affected limb on the proximal side of the damaged tissue only; that is the area nearer to the heart. By treating in this manner you effect lymphatic drainage and reduction of the recalcitrant swelling. Never massage a client with a high temperature or, if he or she has an infectious or contagious disease. Signs of rashes, areas covered with spots, unless diagnosed by a medical practitioner and permission to massage given, are contra-indications. There are some exceptions, such as an allergy;

however, until the cause is found, to massage may further irritate the problem. A golden rule is to decline treatment until the condition is considered safe.

Whilst an arthritic sufferer, with stiff joints can be aided by massage, a badly inflamed area must not be vigorously disturbed, further inflammation could result from this. A fibrositic condition may invariably benefit from a localized friction. Varicose veins and other serious circulatory diseases, must always be avoided; e.g. arteriosclerosis, phlebitis, thrombosis, etc.

Never massage when a wound is discharging pus, or if your client is suspected of suffering from an internal (or external) hæmorrhage. Final caution, NO ATTEMPT must ever be made to massage a person sustaining burns. I repeat 'WHEN IN DOUBT, DON'T.'

The Anatomy of the Hand

The importance of having some understanding of anatomy cannot be over stressed. It is the extremities of the body, such as the arms and legs, that work for us continuously throughout the day. The muscles and tendons of the hands and feet, are small and numerous. All you need to know at this point is never to miss out these important appendages. The muscles mainly extend and flex the limb. Extension flexion, flexion extension. Muscles tend to lie in groups and aid one another in certain defined movements. They are, to put it crudely, the red meat that you see in a butcher's shop. They also afford padding; therefore protecting vital organs or viscera that lie within the physical frame. Treat the body in your care with reverence. Do not race to finish, take pleasure in what you do; there should be no hurry. You could, in all probability, be needed to help competitors in sporting events find the necessary strength with which to compete.

The skeletal hand and arm starts at the wrist; the wrist being composed of eight carpus or carpal bones. Leaving this mosaic pattern of carpals, and continuing in a straight line towards the knuckles, are five metacarpal bones; these form the back of the hand. In each of the fingers there are three phalanges; the thumb has only two. These twenty seven bones form the hand and the wrist. Surrounding the wrist is a cartilaginous band known as an annular ligament, which gives support to the wrist and carpals.

The Anatomy of the Forearm and Arm

The forearm extends from the wrist to the elbow joint; it is composed of two bones, the radius and the ulnar. If you observe the forearm in the anterior aspect, i.e. with the palm of the hand facing the front, the radius is situated on the outside and consequently the ulnar on the inside. The muscles of the forearm are small in structure. Five of the main muscles are as follows: supinator radii longus; external communis digitorum; extensor carpii radialis longus; flexor carpii ulnaris; palmaris longus.

The arm extends from the elbow joint to the shoulder; it consists of a long bone called the humerus. The head of the humerus has a ball-shaped knob or prominence, which fits into the glenoid cavity; a concave space in the scapula or shoulder blade. The upper outside of the arm is covered by the deltoid; this muscle extends to the middle outside of the humerus. The biceps are on the anterior or front aspect of the arm; their action is to supinate and flex the forearm. The triceps are situated on the posterior or back aspect of the arm. They are the extensors, thereby extending the forearm to its fullest limits.

Before involving yourself in the following section, I would like to draw your attention to two anatomical terms that are frequently used. They are 'distal' and 'proximal'. The distal end of a limb is the end that lies furthest from the heart. The proximal end of a limb is the end that lies nearest to the heart.

The Anatomy of the Foot, Leg and Thigh

The skeletal structure of the foot is intricate and comprises twenty six bones: fourteen phalanges, five metatarsals leading to the seven tarsals of the ankle. The leg has two bones; the tibia which is also known as the shin bone, and the fibula, which lies behind the tibia. I will mention only one muscle in the leg; remember that it is below the knee. It is the calf muscle, the gastrocnemius. I feel that as it is very large and constitutes most of the leg, you need concern yourself with no other muscle in this area. This large twin headed muscle, extends the foot and bends the knee.

Now observe the knee joint. The patella is the small triangular key bone positioned in front of the centre of the knee, in between the fibula, tibia and femur. It can be palpated and if the limb is relaxed, a little movement can be felt under your hand. The patella is kept in position mainly by the ligamentum patella. The space at the back of the knee is called the popliteal space.

The femur is the long bone of the thigh. The distal end of the femur forms the top of the knee joint; the proximal end has a small ball-like knob, that fits into the lower end of the pelvis. The recipient cavity is called the acetabulum or hip joint. The ball and socket action of this joint, permits a full range of multidirectional movements to the thigh. Some of the more important muscles of the thigh are as follows. On the posterior aspect, are the three ham-string muscles. They are semimembranosus, semitendinosus, biceps femoris. These muscles are flexors, they flex as well as rotate the leg. On the anterior aspect of the thigh you will find the quadriceps extensors. They do what their name suggests, extend the leg. They are, rectus femoris, vastus internus, vastus medialis (crureus), vastus externus. I will mention one more muscle here that starts on the inside of the thigh above the knee, traversing the leg ending on the outside and proximal end of the thigh. This muscle is the sartorius. It helped the tailors of a bygone age, to sit in their notorious posture. It helps as well as hinders some, who meditate in a position known as the lotus.

The Anatomy of the Body: The Skeletal and Muscular System

For a general picture of the human frame I want you first to visualize the skull, swivel-seated on top of the spine. The following bone structure consists of seven cervical vertebrae situated in the neck. Then twelve dorsal vertebrae; a pair of ribs being attached to each one. Five lumbar vertebrae end the mobile spine. The last of the spinal vertebrae being five sacrum and the coccyx, which constitutes the centre back of the pelvis. The pelvis in turn comprises four innominate bones, which, being welded into an osseous mass, are immovable. The scapulæ or shoulder blades lie on the outside of the posterior higher rib cage. On the upper anterior aspect of the body is the clavicle or collar bone, which articulates with both the sternum and the scapula. The sternum is the breast bone.

Lying obliquely across the neck is the sterno-cleido-mastoideus muscle. Its action is to bend the head forward and to one side. Another important muscle of the neck is the splenius-capitus. It extends the head and neck and also bends the head sideways and backwards. The trapezius covers the scapulæ and shoulders; it is shaped like a kite, the apex pointing downwards towards the last dorsal vertebra. Its action is to move the shoulders up and backwards, also to elevate the arm. The latissimus-dorsi covers the lumbar vertebrae and the outer dorsal region. This muscle pulls the elevated arm in a backward and downward direction; extending as well as rotating the arm inwards. On each side of the spine lie the erector spinæ muscles occupying the whole length of the spine. Their action is to keep the spine erect and extended. Now we come to the gluteus-maximus, medius and minimus muscles, which fortunately for us, afford padding when we sit down. These seat-muscles give various actions to the thighs.

In between each pair of ribs are the intercostal muscles that aid the respiration. Slightly higher and in front are the pectoralis major muscles which draw the arms across the chest, as well as giving lift to the bosom. Covering the whole length of the abdomen is the rectus abdominus. This muscle helps with the expiration. There are somewhere in the region of five hundred muscles housed in the human body. I have mentioned a very few and then only briefly, so start by only concerning yourself with the muscles you will actually handle. The interested reader will find fully comprehensive works available in most book shops of repute or in the public library.

The Anatomy of the Body: The Circulatory System

The circulatory system is sometimes referred to as the vascular-system. It is a circuit which has the heart for its centre. That pump of all pumps sends life, in the form of oxygenated blood, to all living cells and organs in the body, at the same time dealing with stale used blood, sending it in turn through the lungs to be re-oxygenated. This is, of course, an over-simplification of a complex system of blood distribution.

The circulation is dealt with by the heart, the arteries, capillaries, veins and lymphatics. Life's fluid is blood. It consists of a multitude of red corpuscles (erythrocytes), and white corpuscles (leucocytes). The red cells are the oxygen-carrying-agents distributing their valuable cargo to the most remote corners of the human empire. The white corpuscles are the body's front line defence army. They die for us in their millions daily. Any invasion of bacteria, such as may be found in an open wound, is immediately set upon by these faithful leucocytes. They die forming pus, which is then exuded from the wound.

Now to take things in turn. The heart is laterally divided, the left arterial side containing pure blood, the right side containing the venous, or impure blood. The heart is sub-divided again, only this time horizontally. The upper compartments are known as auricles or atria and the lower, ventricles. The blood leaves the heart by the aorta artery which is situated in the left ventricle. It then continues under pressure to all parts of the body; finally to return by the various veins, being emptied into the venæ cavæ and then the heart once more.

The arteries and veins are connected by capillaries. These are a miniscule network of hair-like vessels that receive the blood and pass on its nutriments to adjacent cells. The blood loses its oxygen content, becoming laden with the body's impurities. This neutral coloured fluid, lymph, is then carried towards the lymph glands in order to be filtered. There are a number of these glands in the body, especially in the neck, armpit and the groin. The lymph is then conveyed into the thoracic or into the right lymphatic duct, then back to the heart. Lymph absorbs waste; its purpose is to carry away such effete matter from the body's tissues. The veins have valves which stop the blood from running back. There is a constant interchange between lymphatic fluid and blood; this process of absorption is known as osmosis.

For anyone practising massage, it is important to understand that the systematic compression of the bodies' tissues, as practised in massage, is a most effective method of encouraging lymphatic circulation. It is a definite aid in eliminating waste and accumulative toxins from the body with beneficial consequences.

The Movements of Massage

In the next part of this book you will be invited to participate in actual body massage. Before you can start doing the exercises it will be necessary to understand something of the movements you will be required to make. There are four: EFFLEURAGE: PETRISSAGE: FRICTION: TAPOTEMENT.

Effleurage is a stroking movement: it can be done with the flat of the hand, the fingers alone, or, in conjunction with the thumbs. Its application may be light or heavy. Its object is to aid venous return and to restore muscle tone.

Petrissage is the act of lifting, separating or wringing out of muscle in groups or singly. The fingers and thumbs pick up, then separate muscle tissue. Both hands are usually required to perform this movement. To knead a muscle is to give petrissage; in fact both effleurage and petrissage can knead. It is a borderline movement.

Friction is a penetrating search in depth, usually made with the thumbs. It can also be applied with the finger tips, quite often by one finger buttressing another to give extra pressure. One thinks of friction being most effective when breaking down acid crystals that are reputed to form under the skin and muscles, then allowing the circulation to wash away the debris. It can also be applied with the flat of both hands rubbing the skin in alternate directions so as to promote heat.

Tapotement is the art of percussion when the percussed object is the body. There are various forms of percussion. Classically one tends to think of a person being chopped with the leading edge of the masseur's hands in quick succession. This is known as hacking and is but one of many variations of tapotement. Cupping is another facet of percussion; it consists of forming one's hands into dome shaped mounds, then hitting lightly and quickly on a naturally-formed cushion of air. Pounding with the fist very lightly clenched is yet another variant, as well as beating, and so forth. These movements of tapotement are either liked or disliked. They are not made deeply and being superficial, stimulate the skin and immediate underlying tissue only.

There are however, many variations to all of the four basic movements which are usually classified under one of the given headings. The art of massage is to be able to permutate movements, applying the right amount of pressure for the correct duration. Certainly be enthusiastic, allowing a word of advice here: always fully understand what it is that you are trying to do as well as why; then do it!

Massage of the Upper Extremities

Firstly it is necessary for your client to remove all or most of his or her clothes. Some people, depending upon the mental and physical climate, prefer nudity. Either way a large towel is placed at the foot of your plinth to be used as required. The plinth should already be covered with a sheet or towel on which to lie. Do not forget to place a small thin pillow at the head of the couch. Should your client be female, then also provide a small towel with which to cover the bosom. Your client's feelings must be considered and to omit these first refinements may produce unnecessary tension which would inhibit the establishment of a rapport. The preliminaries before commencing the massage, need especial thought and attention; e.g. it is good policy, should you not have a screen, to leave the room whilst your client undresses and adjusts him- or herself on the couch. Your hands should of course be free of watches, rings etc. To wash them in *warm* water is an obvious advantage. At this stage you require an oil bottle, preferably one with a small aperture such as found in some shampoo bottles, containing your choice of oil. Remember to massage whenever possible in the direction of the heart. The following is the sequence that you should follow. Start by giving massage to the left hand, then the forearm and arm, proceeding to the left foot. After completing the leg and the thigh, continue around the body in a clockwise direction, repeating your movements of massage to the right foot, leg and thigh. Now move to your client's right hand and arm. Massage as you will be instructed and finish your movements by covering the area treated with a towel. Each of the upper and lower extremities (arms and legs), will take you somewhere in the region of five minutes per limb; this accumulates to a twenty minute time schedule. Do not feel obliged to stick rigidly to this, use it only as a guide.

Procedure
With your client lying supine, i.e. on his or her back, position yourself on your client's left hand side. Pour a little oil into your hands and transfer this on to the front and back surfaces of your client's hand, which should now be in a vertical position. (See figure number 1.) This illustration indicates the ideal position for this movement. Should you have poured too much oil, spread the surplus onto the client's forearm. Now proceed by giving massage to each finger in turn including the thumb. Direct your movements from the distal towards the proximal end, which is where the fingers join the hand. Continue by giving effleurage to the hand as a whole using a kneading and friction action with your thumbs to the palm. (See figure number 2a.) Hold the hand as in the figure illustrations above and try to manipulate the wrist so as to cause the hand to complete a full range of movements. Do this gently and avoid being abrupt. Return the hand and forearm to the rest position on the couch.

With both of your hands, proceed to hold firmly your client's forearm; try if you can to hold the muscles only. They lie on the inside forearm. (See figure number 2b.) You may achieve this by standing close to the plinth, supporting the outside surface of the arm against your thigh. The muscles in this area although five in number, are not very bulky, therefore you may find it a little difficult to accomplish this manipulation. Give petrissage, i.e. lifting and kneading these muscles, then flex the limb so that the hand reaches the shoulder. While in the vertical position, (See figure number 3), effleurage and return the arm to the rest position.

Proceed to the biceps (twin-headed muscles situated on the inside arm above the elbow). Apply slow-rhythmic effleurage followed by petrissage; do likewise to the triceps, (the three-headed muscle situated opposite the biceps on the outside arm). To effect a good movement with the triceps, it will be found advantageous if you turn your back to an angle of 45° to your client (see figure number 4). Stand with your back close to the couch so that you are slightly turned towards the head. Now whilst in this position, endeavour to pick up the muscle in between your fingers and thumbs of both hands; knead. Correct positioning of your body can be used to your advantage in massage. Effleurage the rest of the arm which will automatically include the deltoid, a muscle of the upper arm. Now effleurage the whole of the arm, forearm and hand, right up to the shoulder in sweeping movements. Several measured movements like this, being performed smoothly and slowly, will complete massage to the upper extremity. Cover the limb with a towel so as to conserve heat resulting in a relaxed arm. May I emphasise that one should always start and finish your massage movements to any area of the body with effleurage. It is also important to remember to maintain contact with the body whilst changing position and in between movements. Ease will come with practice.

You may hear some authorities formulate the opinion that this method of massage takes too long and that it involves unnecessary detail. Do not be persuaded to miss out important areas of the body, or to rush the treatment; you, fortunately are not working on a factory conveyor-belt! This book with its appropriate suggestions, is for your benefit: the ideas were gained through experience. Now proceed to the left foot.

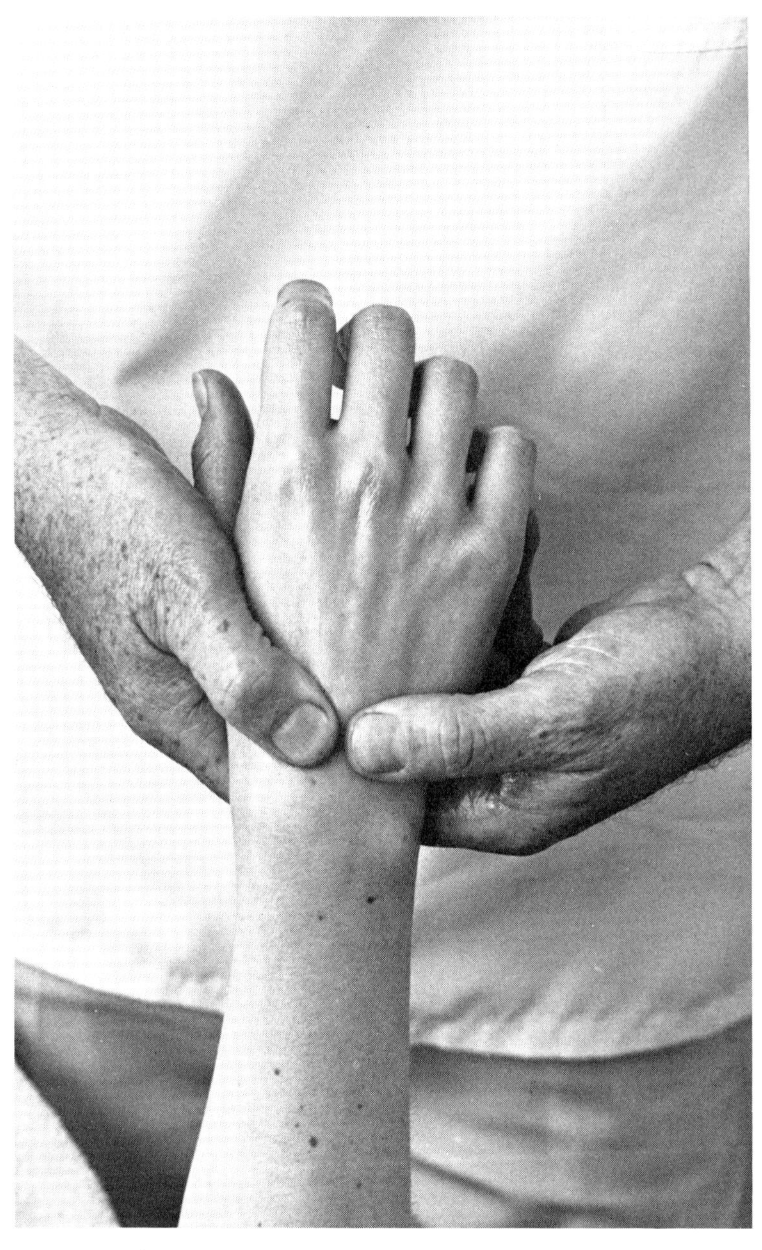

FIG. 1 *Manipulating the Metacarpals from the Knuckles to the Wrist*

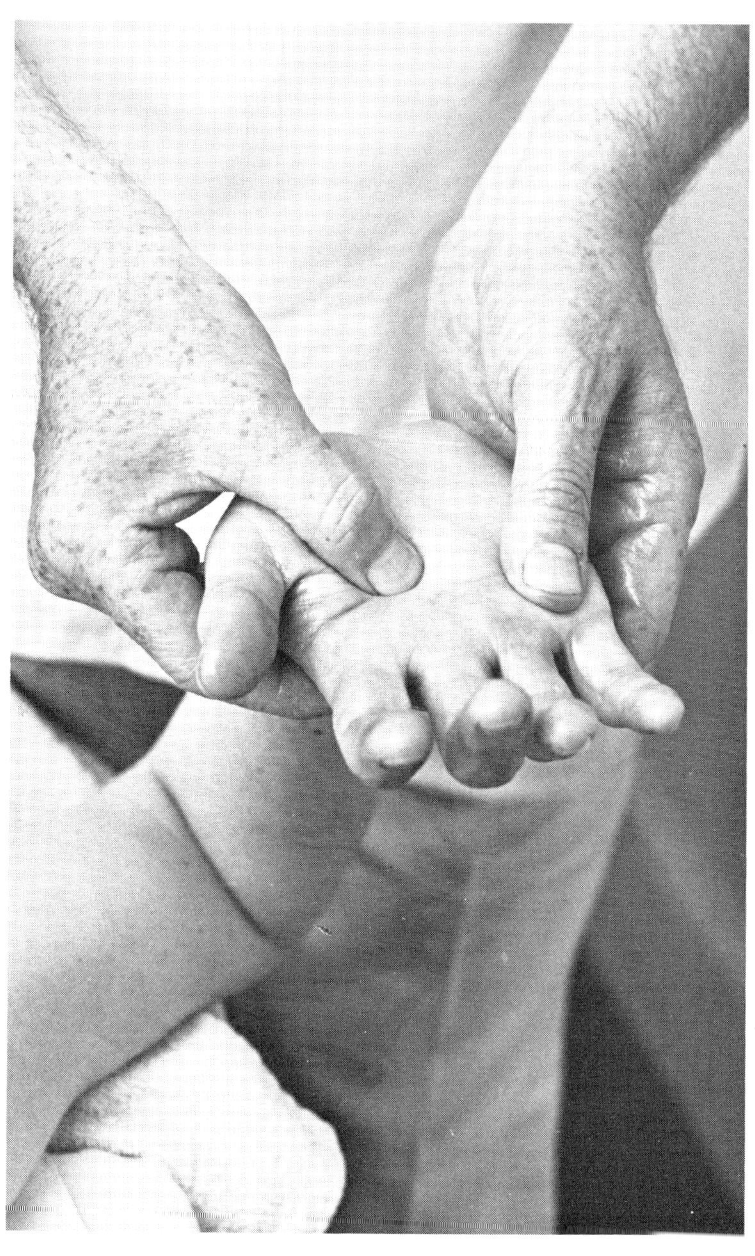

FIG. 2a *Kneading the Palmar Surface of the Hand*

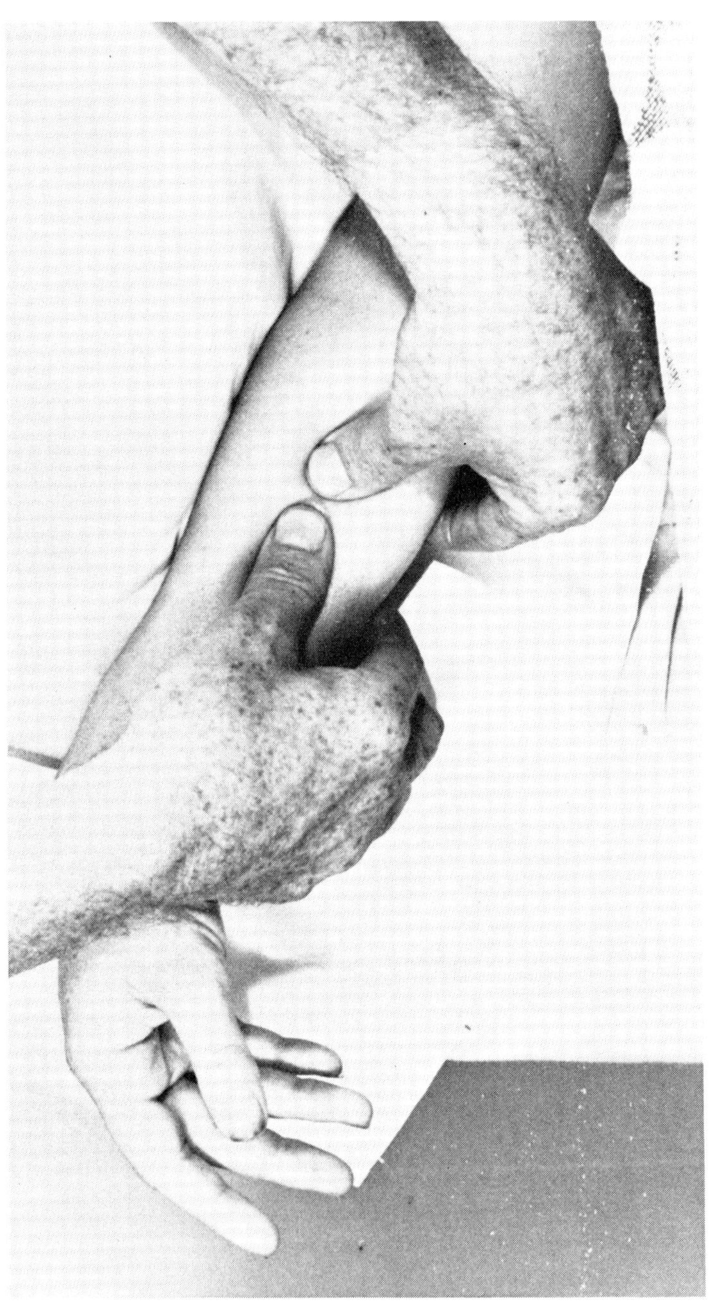

FIG. 2b *Petrissage to the Forearm*

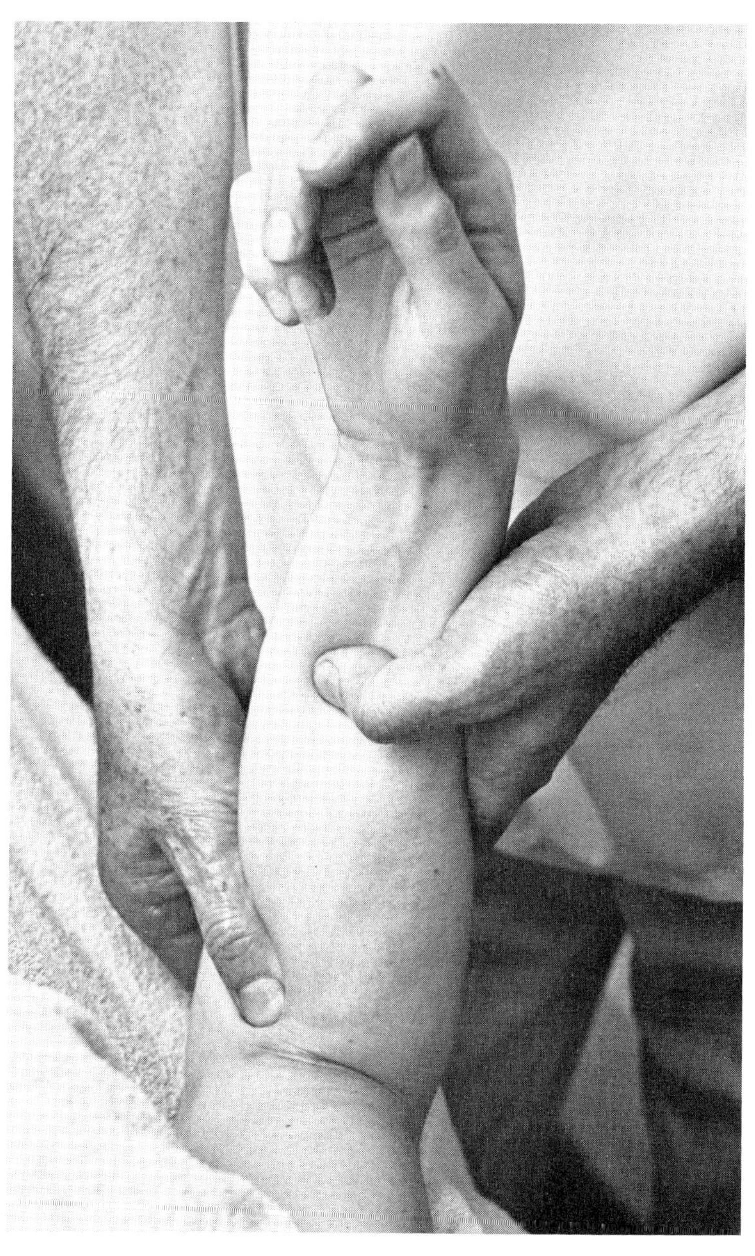

FIG. 3 *Effleurage to the Forearm*

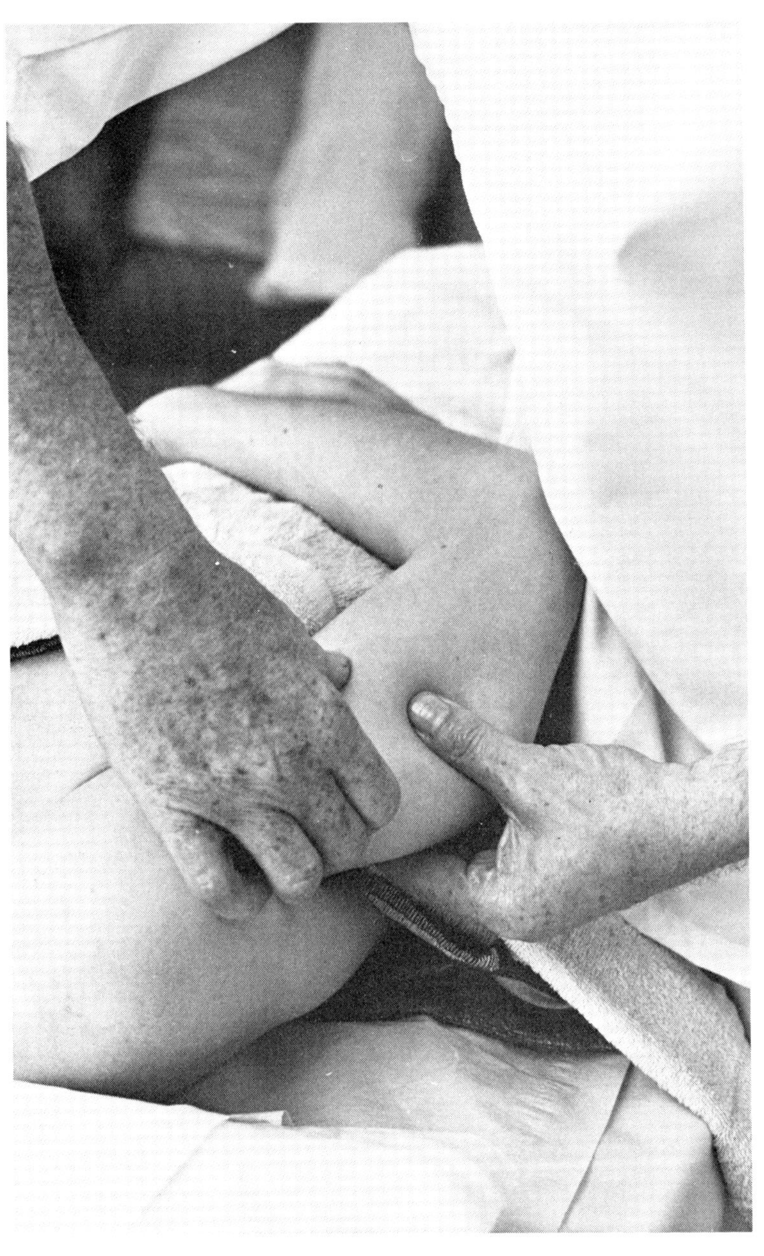

FIG. 4 *Applying Petrissage to the Triceps*

Massage of the Lower Extremities

The foot can sometimes be ultra-sensitive to touch, therefore, after pouring oil into your hands, proceed by taking hold of the left foot firmly. A firm gentle pressure to the plantar arch (the underneath area), and upper surface of the foot for about 20 seconds, will convey a feeling of unspoken confidence; it feels good. Effleurage the upper and under surfaces of the foot so as to distribute the oil evenly over the whole area. (See figure numbers 5, 6 and 7.) Effleurage the toes, then the metatarsals; remember, the five bones in the structure of the foot and finally, the foot as a whole. Allow your fingers to intrude gently in the slight depression at the back of the ankle on both sides of the foot. You are now in the proximity of the achilles tendon, the key note being gentle massage as there is not very much muscle at this position. Now manipulate the foot through a full range of movements, a gentle persuasive bending, and proceed without pause to the leg.

Give effleurage to the leg, i.e. from the ankle to the knee and after a few rhythmic strokes, place your forearm under the knee and fully raise the leg, keeping it in this position. (See figure numbers 8 and 9.) You are now in a good position to work on the gastrocnemius or calf-muscle. Try using both of your hands, knead and effleurage the muscle in an upward direction until it responds to your touch becoming more pliable. Finally, replace the leg in its former position on the couch.

Now proceed to the knee. With your fingers and thumbs encircle the patella (the knee cap). (See figure numbers 10 and 11.) A gentle circumnavigation of this floating key bone will ensure that it has freedom of movement. A number of gentle movements here are all that is needed.

Proceed to the thigh and cover completely with oil. Apply effleurage as well as petrissage over this well muscle-populated limb. I will try to convey to you my own method of doing this. Start at the distal end of the thigh just above the knee. Distribute the oil evenly with the flat of your hands, working towards the proximal end where the thigh joins the trunk. It is well to point out here that your hands should mould to the contours of the limb being treated. Give petrissage to the vastus externus, a specific muscle on the outside thigh (see figure number 12a), draw your fingers firmly with an even pressure along the whole length of this muscle, the emphasis being on the centre outside thigh, holding the muscle in between your thumb and fingers, then do likewise to the rectus femoris, a muscle situated on the anterior aspect of the thigh (see figure number 12b). Repeat this three times, returning your hands lightly to the distal end of the muscle without losing contact with the body. It is important however, that the return movement of the hands should always be accomplished without pressure being exerted. Now find the approximate position of the sartorius (the lower inside thigh just above the knee). Follow the course of this muscle as it traverses the thigh in an oblique deflection finishing on the upper outside of the thigh. Progress by repeating this kneading movement with your fingers and thumbs several times, with each movement progressing higher up the inside thigh. Now clasp the whole of the limb, one hand on either side with the finger tips touching on the upper surface of the thigh just above the knee. Allow your hands to traverse the limb from the knee to the top of the thigh, returning lightly each time to the starting point close to the knee. This can be performed three times. If you can visualise the next part of the movement, it will become an interesting deviation. Complete the first part of the movement as above and as your hands return to the knee area, reverse the position of the fingers so that the fingers this time will be around the outside of the thigh with the thumbs on top. Now apply massage to the thigh alternating the hand position with each movement, firstly with your fingers on the upper surface and then repeating with your thumbs in the superior position. The pressures will alternate pleasantly and effectively. Finish the limb with effleurage. Cover and proceed to the right foot, leg and thigh; repeat the previous movements. Now having completed the anterior or front aspect of the lower extremities, proceed to the right hand, forearm and arm and massage these as per previous instructions.

Should any of the above movements prove difficult to accomplish, do not worry too much, as with practice you will eventually achieve what you are endeavouring to do. The next section will deal with the neck; chest (should your client be male), and the abdomen.

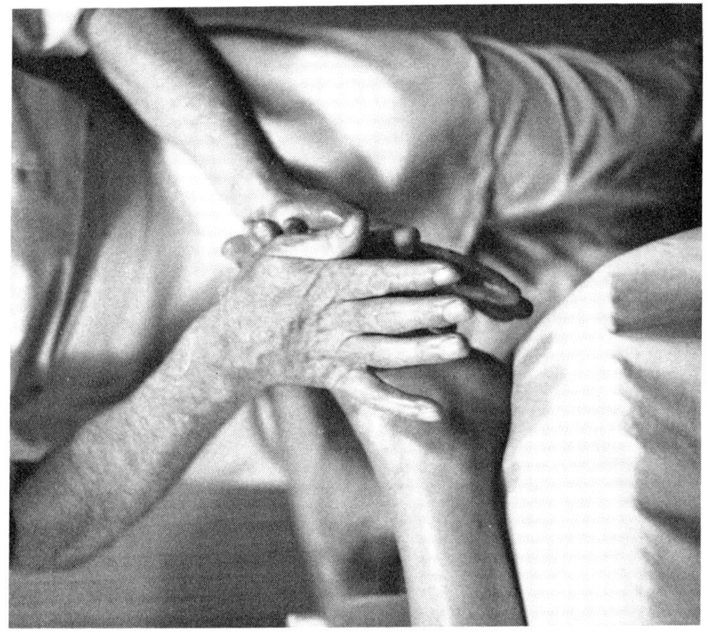

FIG. 6 *Applying Friction to the Toes*

FIG. 5 *Kneading the Metatarsals*

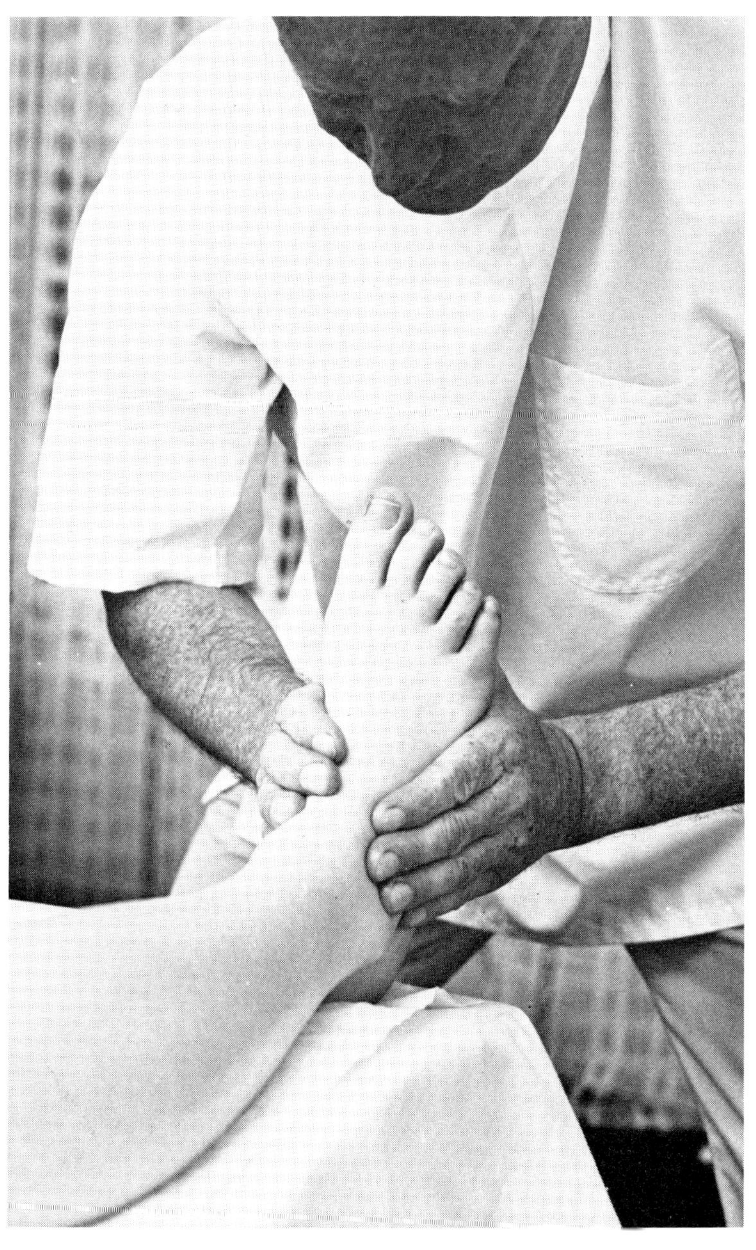

FIG. 7 *Effleurage to the Upper Surface of the Foot*

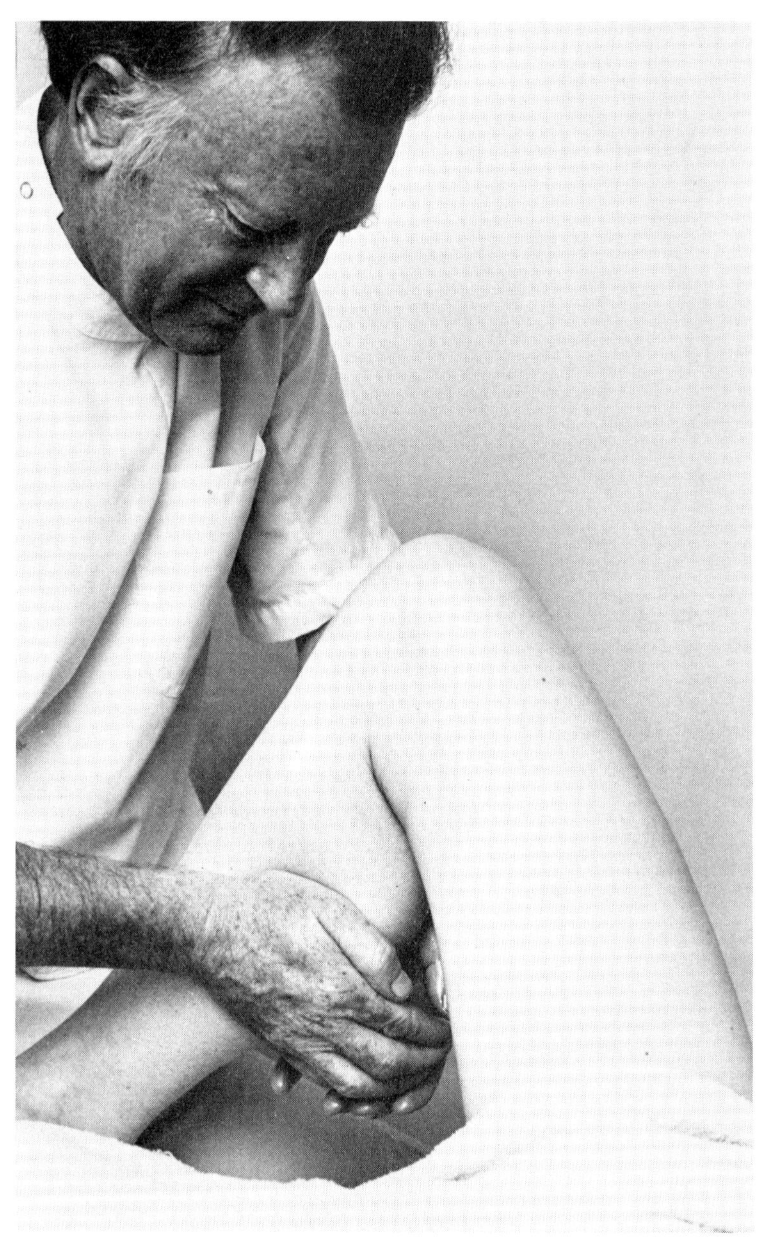

FIG. 8 *Kneading the Calf Muscles of the Leg*

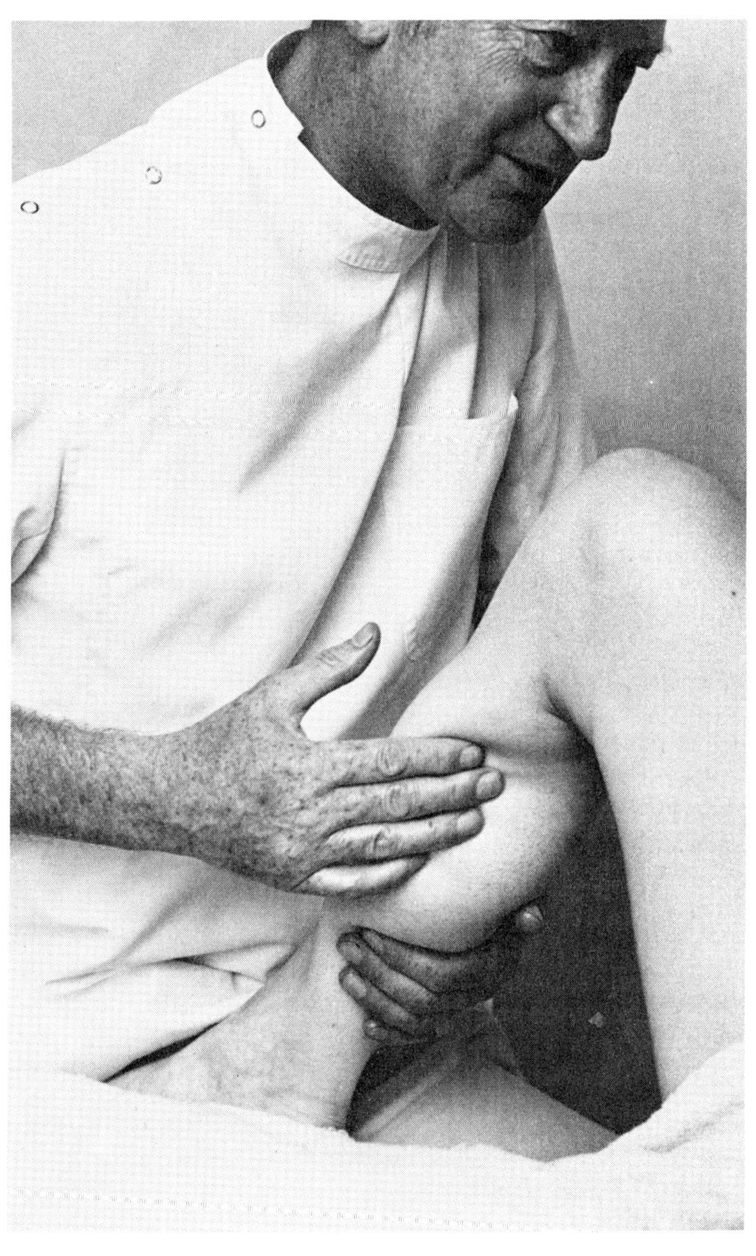

FIG. 9 *Kneading the Calf Muscles of the Leg*

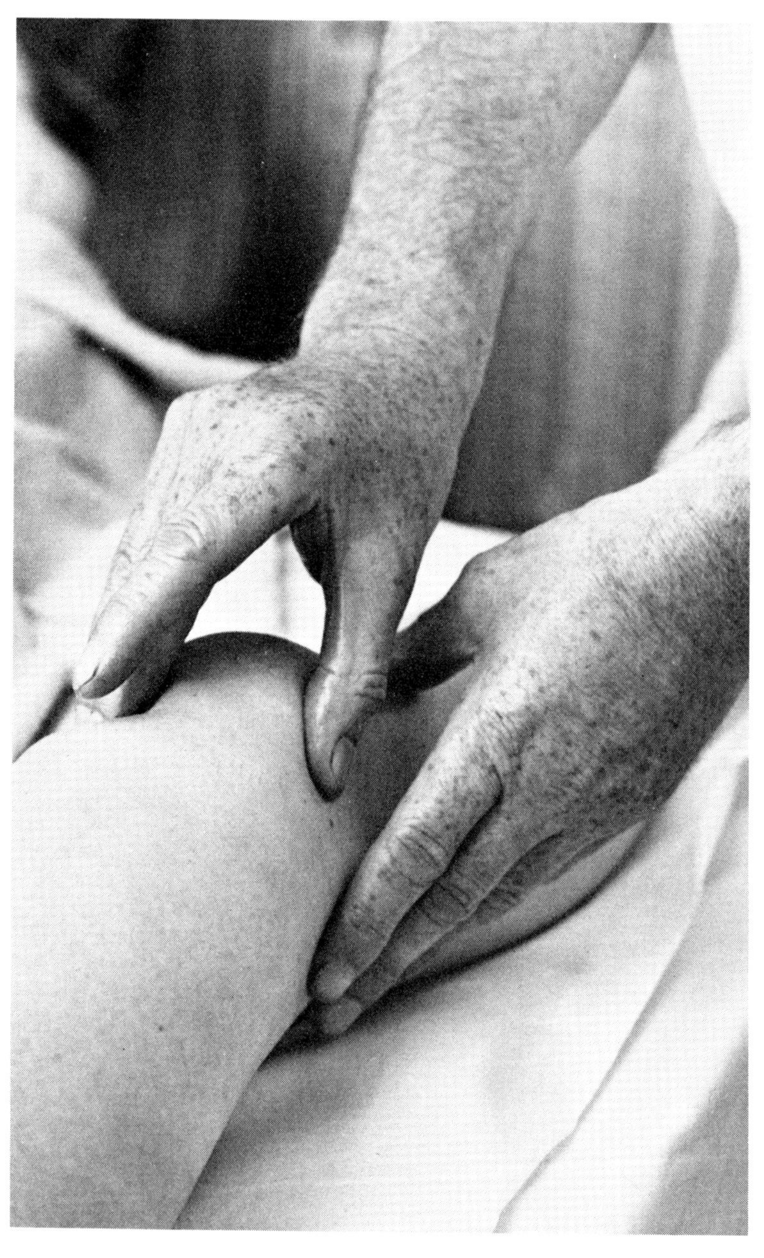

Fig. 10 *Manipulation to the Knee*

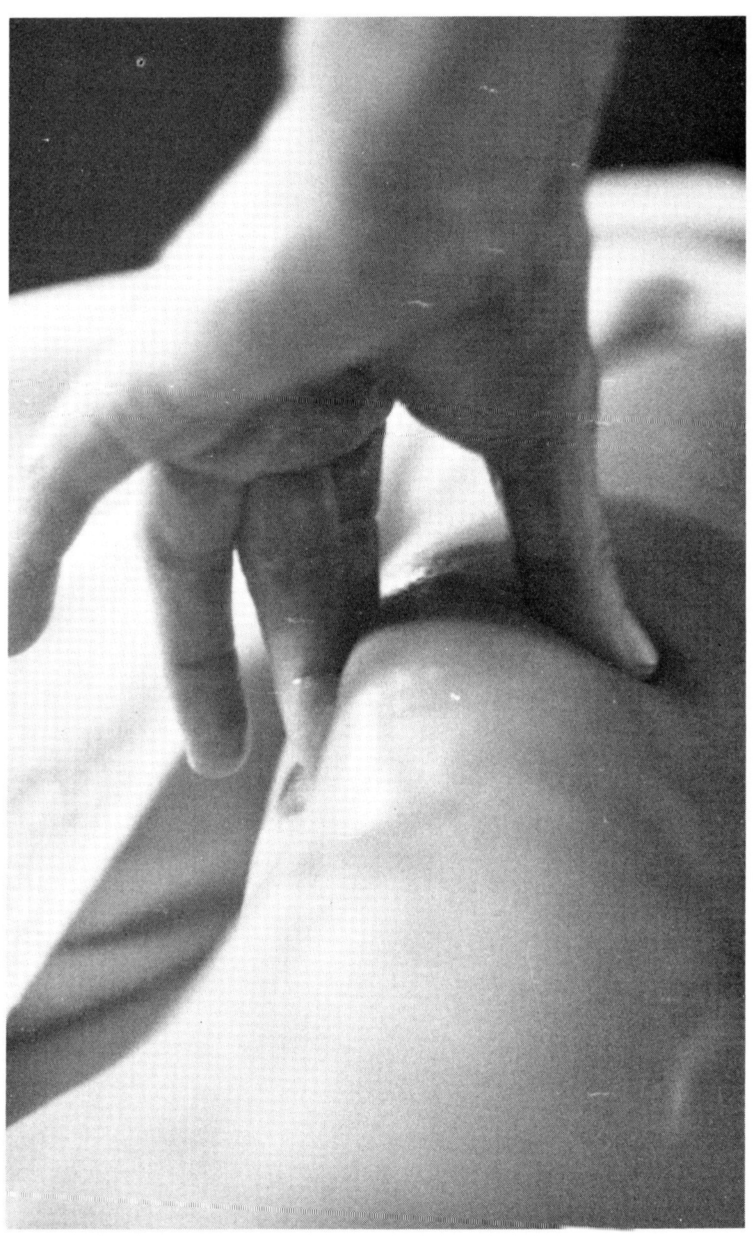

Fig. 11 *Palpating the Patella*

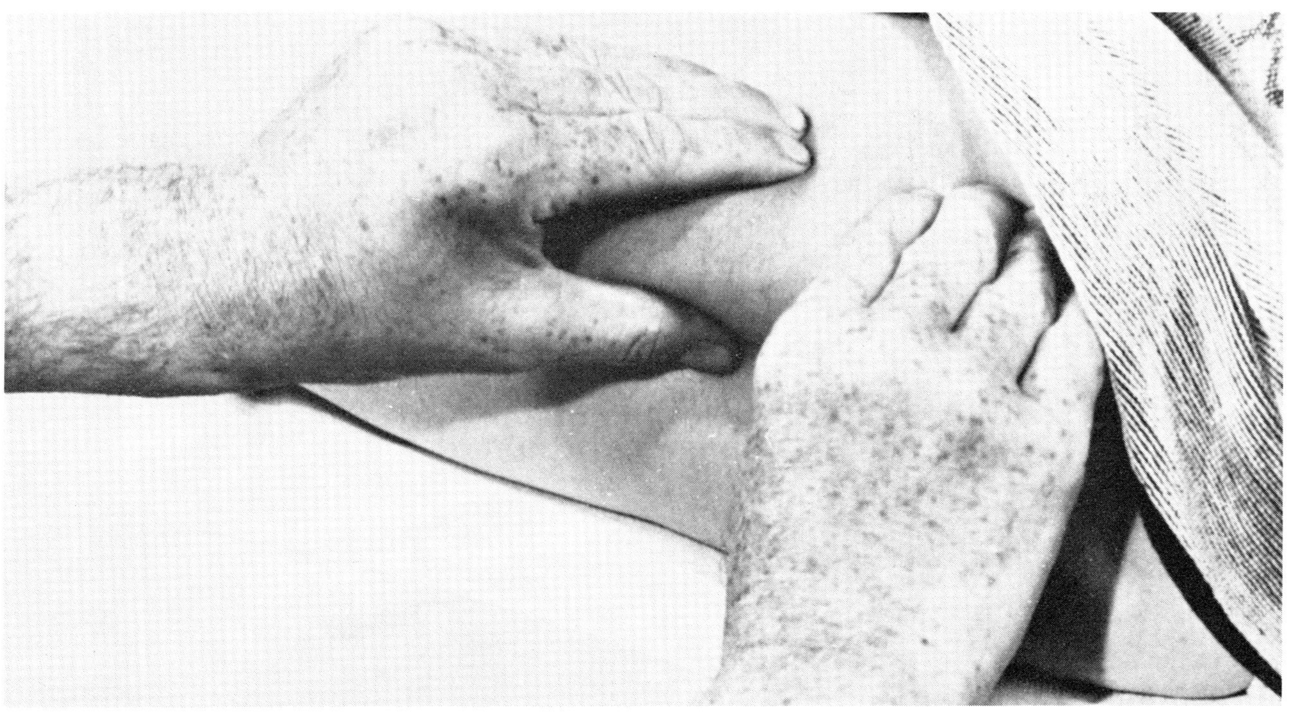

FIG. 12a *Petrissage to the Vastus Externus*

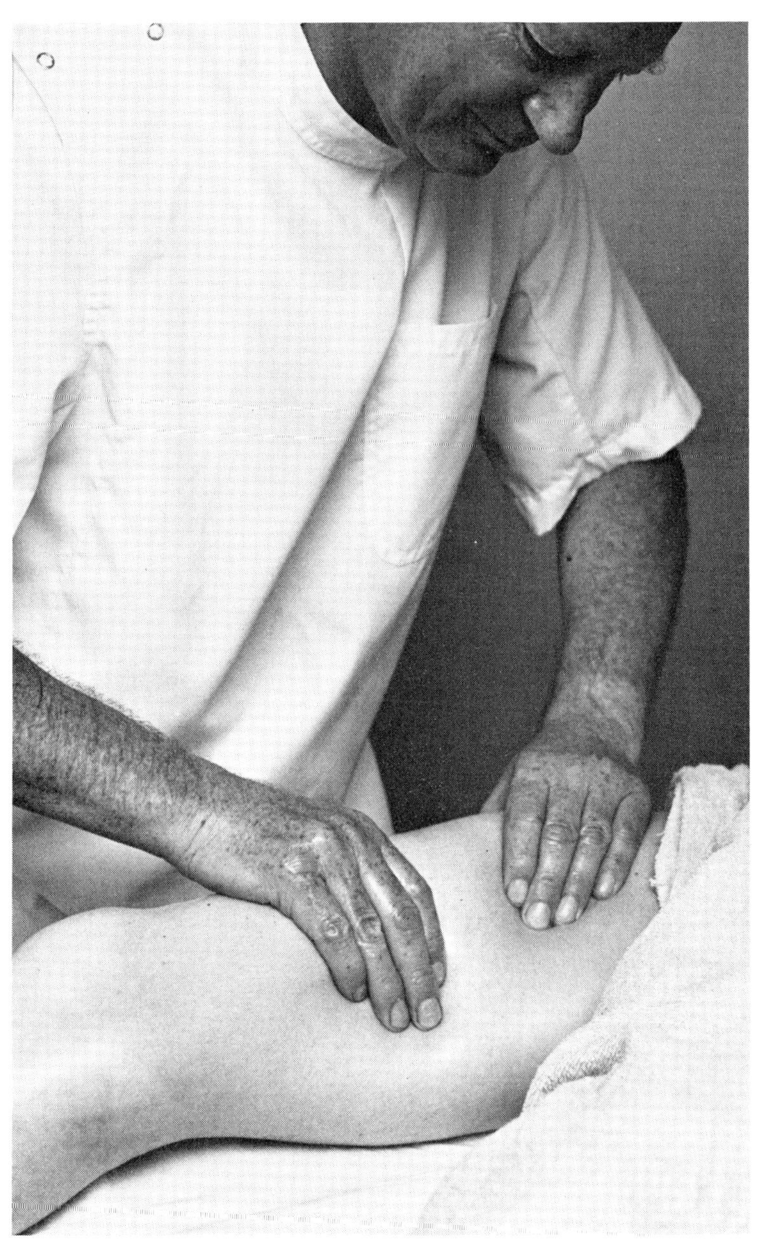

FIG. 12b *Applying Petrissage to the Thigh Muscles*

Massage of the Neck, Chest and Abdomen

I would like you to remain on your client's right hand side; in fact in the same position in which you find yourself upon completing the right arm. For future reference I will speak of the left or right hand side, as meaning your client's left or right side. This will of course be the opposite to your left and right when you are facing your client's head. Now apply oil gently to the whole of the neck. Pressure must on NO ACCOUNT be exerted on the anterior or front aspect of the neck. By using your thumbs or fingers, whichever you can work with best, I would like you now to give friction to each side of the neck. Apply your friction movements in small circles, gently and in an upward direction, finishing just below the ears. Finger tip effleurage is also very good here. Repeat these movements several times, then place the back of the hands (see figure numbers 13 and 14), in contact with, and on, each side of the neck. Allow your hands to rotate applying a little intuitive pressure during this movement. If you can, try to accomplish a double movement here. This is achieved as follows. After having completed the hand rotation one way, return your hands to their original position by keeping your fingers in contact with the back of the neck, effecting light effleurage. Repeat this movement three times; do not hurry. Allow your lightly oiled hands to continue effleurage from your client's right shoulder to the left, and vice versa on the upper front chest. Repeat this movement two or three times. Insert your fingers with a gentle persuasive pressure, into the slight depressions immediately above and below the clavicle (collar bone). (See figure number 15.) To give a longer as well as really excellent massage to the neck, move to the head of the couch. Then place your hands on either side of the base of the neck, reaching with the finger tips of both hands, towards your client's scapulæ (shoulder blades). Insinuate your hands under the shoulders, with the fingers resting on each side of the spine. Now in this position, slide your hands upwards, lifting the neck and head slightly off the couch finishing this movement at the base of the skull. Repeat two or three times slowly; this is a good movement. You may, if you wish, do the whole of the neck massage from this position; each has its advantages.

For the next few minutes, let us assume that your client is male. Uncover the chest and apply oil to the whole area. Some people are hirsute by nature, and it will be necessary to use more oil than for a hairless person. Failure to recognize this need for a liberal amount of oil, could lead to a painful experience for the client. Remember that he is in your care and you should have previously asked him to inform you the moment the massage becomes uncomfortable; most people have the common sense to do this, but beware, it takes all types to make a world! Continue by applying effleurage to the chest without concentrating too long in this area. The muscles that you affect here are surface muscles only, however, they should not be overlooked. Massage in an upward direction, returning your hands with a light movement to the bottom of the rib cage. During these movements you should treat the whole of the chest. Deep massage is not advocated.

Before continuing, a little more anatomical knowledge is needed. Most people refer to the abdomen as the stomach. This is understandable but incorrect. Clinically, the stomach is but one of many delicate viscera that are housed in the abdomen; the liver, pancreas, spleen, to name but three. The part of the anatomy that I wish to draw your attention to is the colon. The colon is in fact the large intestine. It is a very busy pipeline, carrying waste matter that is of no further use to the system. Many ailments are caused by the sluggish action of this 'waste disposal unit'. It consists of the ascending, transverse and descending colon. (See figure number 16.) The muscular action of the colon is peristaltic. Peristalsis is the contractions that are made by a snake's body when in movement. The œsophagus (the tube from the mouth to the stomach), the stomach and the intestines are all activated by peristalsis.

To massage the abdomen, remain on your client's right hand side: make sure that your client's legs are raised and if possible supported. The pillow or roll mentioned earlier will now begin to make sense to you. You will note that by raising the legs and thighs, the muscles of the abdomen relax to a marked degree. Now apply effleurage to the abdomen in a clockwise direction. After a minute or so, when you have promoted a feeling of confidence in your client, place your hands on the lower right side of the abdomen – the side that is nearest to you. (See figure numbers 17 and 18.) You are now in the proximity of the ascending colon, so start by giving effleurage, followed by gentle friction to that area: small concentric circles clockwise in direction, the movement of the hands progressing upwards until they reach the rib cage. (See figure numbers 19, 20 and 21.) Continue frictions so as to traverse the abdomen, trying to keep in the proximity of the colon throughout this movement ending on the opposite side of the upper abdomen. Start friction on the descending colon, continuing until you reach the lower abdomen. Your client's descending colon is opposite and away from you. Remain stationary throughout the whole of this procedure. Persevere as it is of paramount importance to get this movement right. Remember to start on your client's right hand side proceeding to his left. Repeat this movement to the whole of the colon twice; up, across, down and once more effleurage the whole of the abdomen in a clockwise direction. Some abdomens are enlarged so as an alternative the use of the forearm is recommended as shown in figure number 22. Before completing abdominal massage, do a little more handwork to the waistline, deep kneading followed by effleurage is recommended here. Apply a final effleurage and then cover the abdomen and chest. Remember, should your client be female, the bosom will already have been covered with a small towel. Lean across the plinth taking hold of the top and bottom outside edge of the towel that is covering your client. Draw the towel towards you holding it up, thus forming a screen giving your client the privacy to turn over in preparation for massage to the back. Now cover your client completely with the towel.

As a point of interest, the abdomen is divided into nine regions. In line with the lower rib cage are the left and right hypochondriac zones, with the epigastric in the middle. Next is the umbilical, with the left and right lumbar on either side. Lastly the hypogastric, which covers the bladder, with the left and right iliac zone on either side. It is not essential that you remember this.

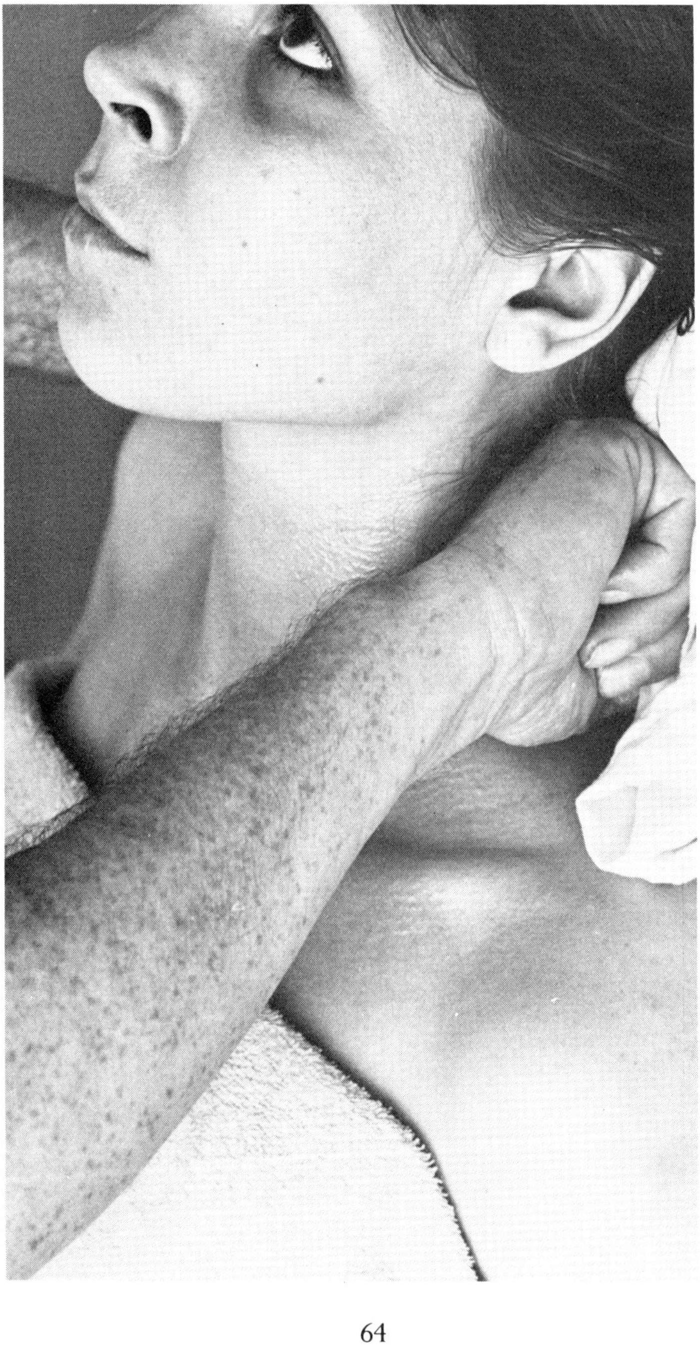

Fig. 13 *Rolling the Hands on the Neck Muscles, 1st Position*

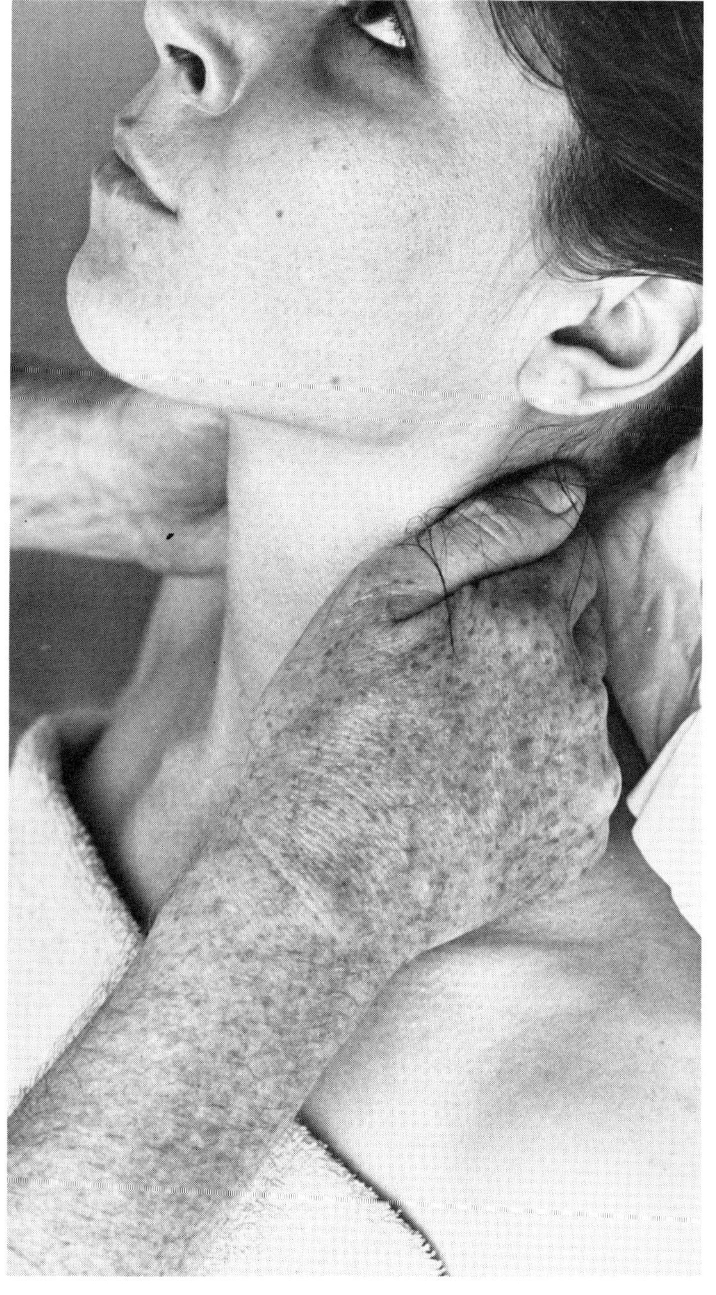

FIG. 14 *Massage to the Neck, 2nd Position*

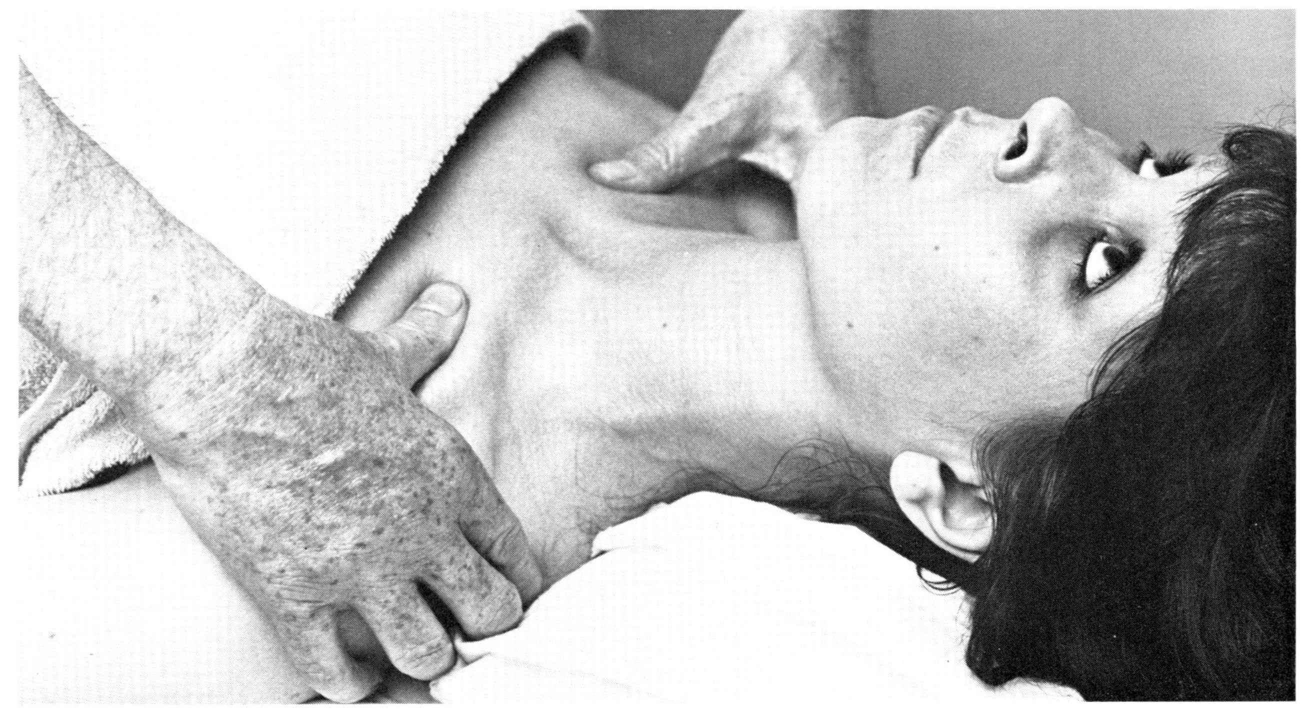

Fig. 15 *Applying Light Pressure along the Inner and Outer Surfaces* of the Collar Bone

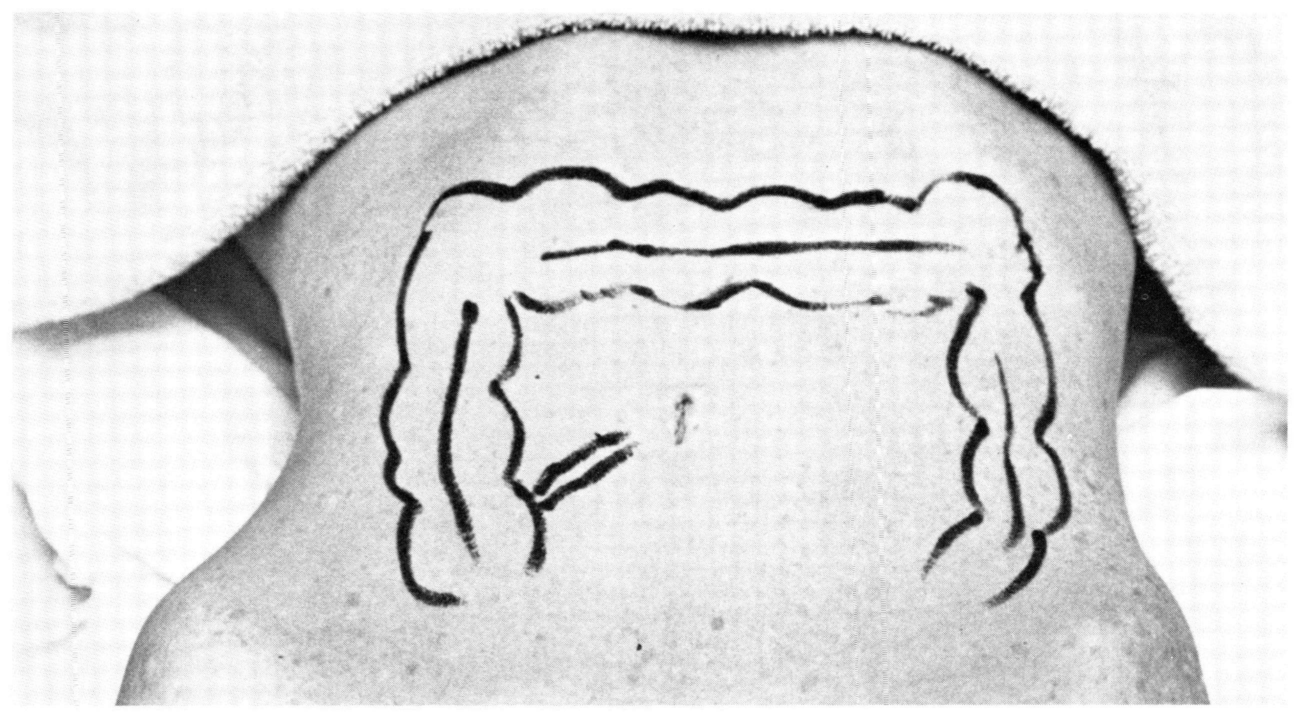

FIG. 16 *The Colon, Slightly Exaggerated, Depicting the Ascending, Transverse and Descending Aspects*

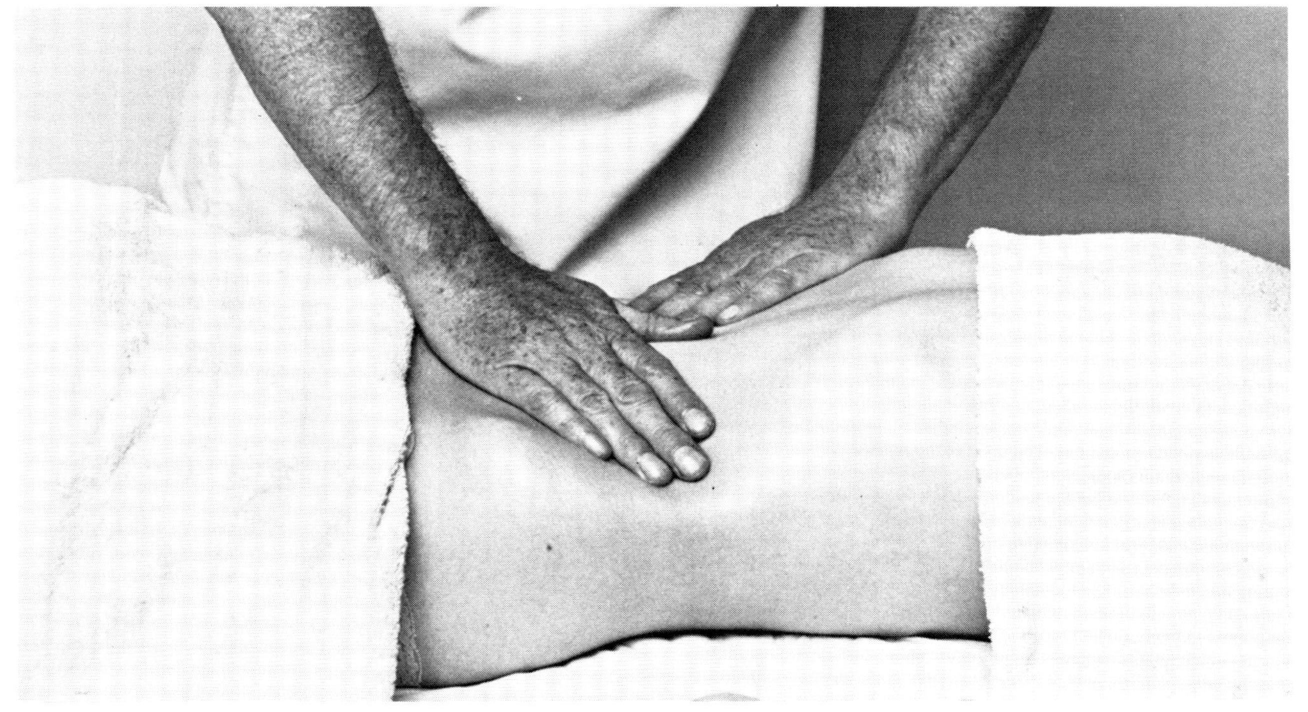

FIG. 17 *Effleurage to the Abdomen*

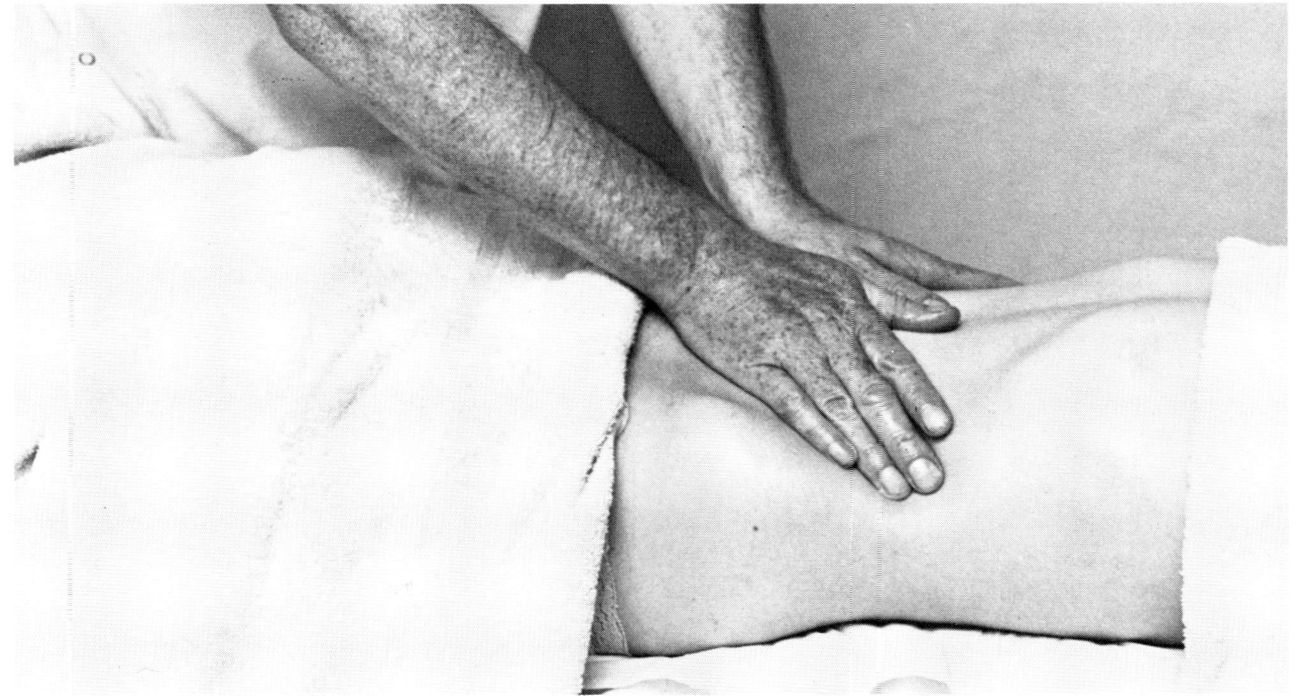

FIG. 18 *Effleurage to the Abdomen*

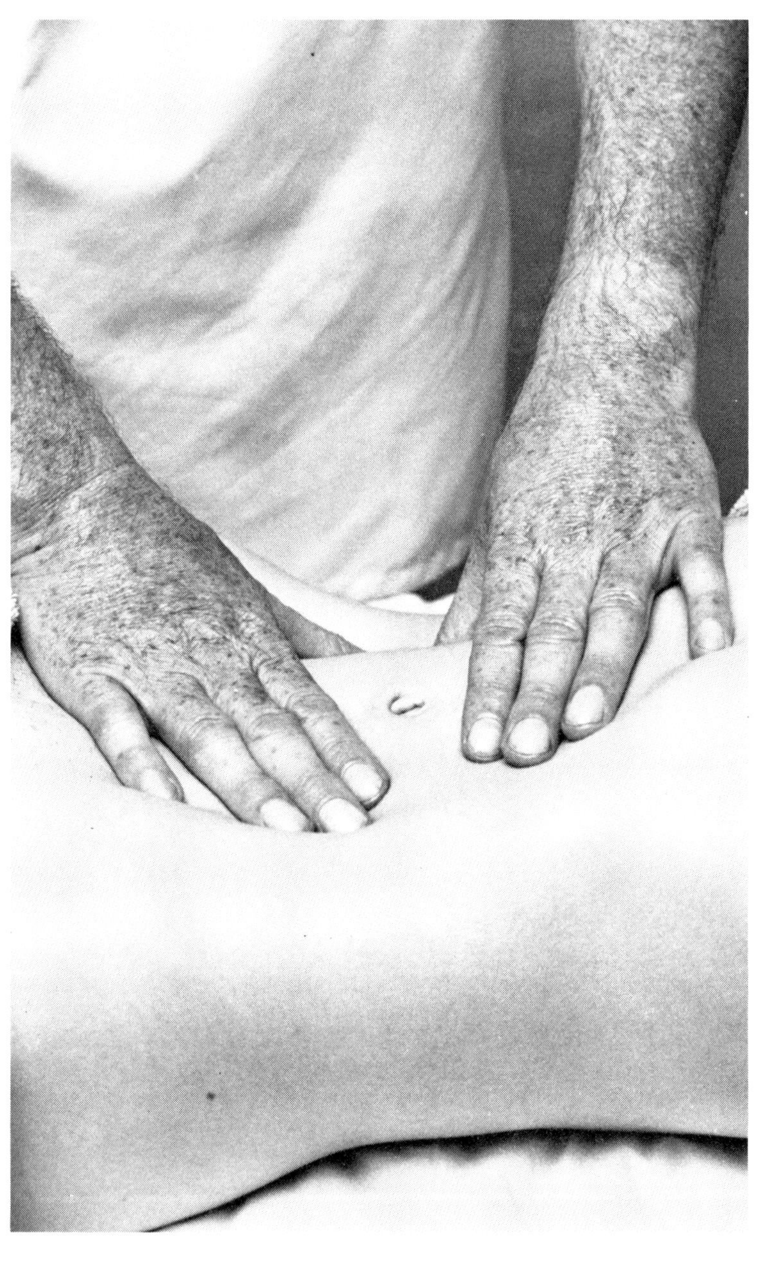

FIG. 19 *Friction to the Ascending Colon*

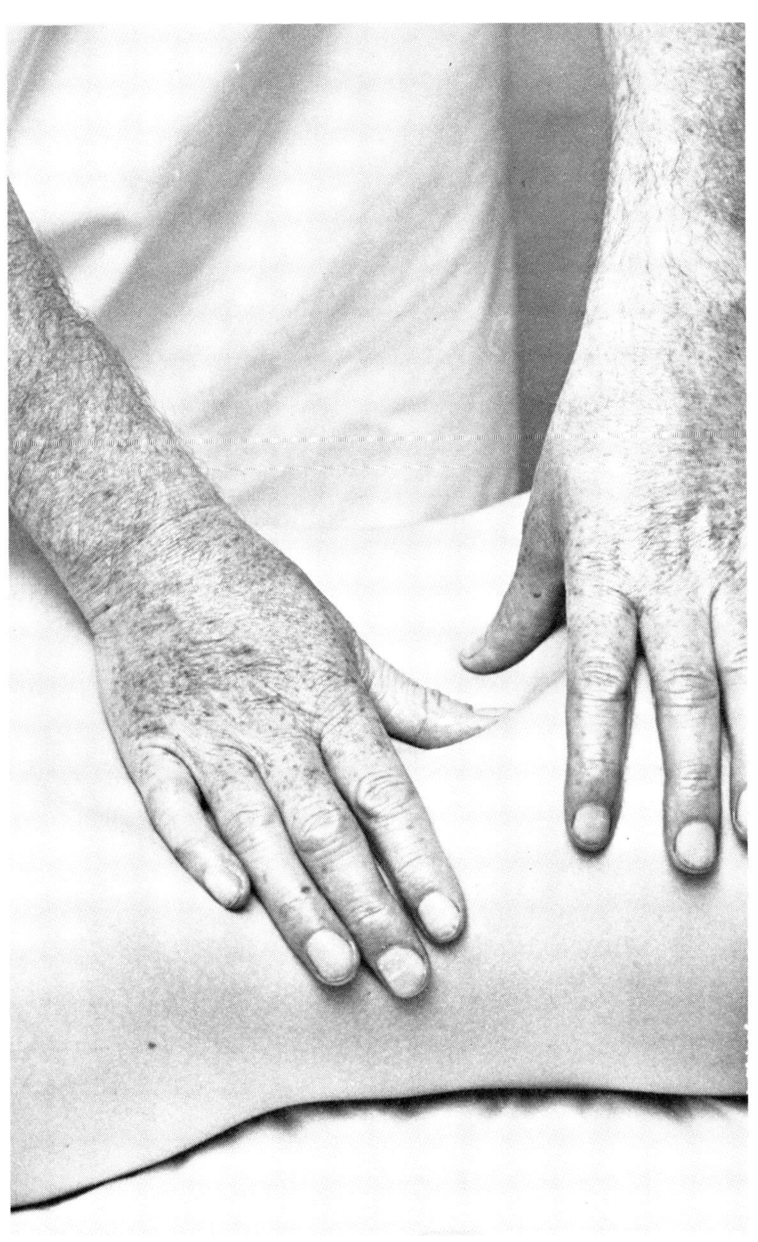

FIG. 20 *Friction to the Transverse Colon*

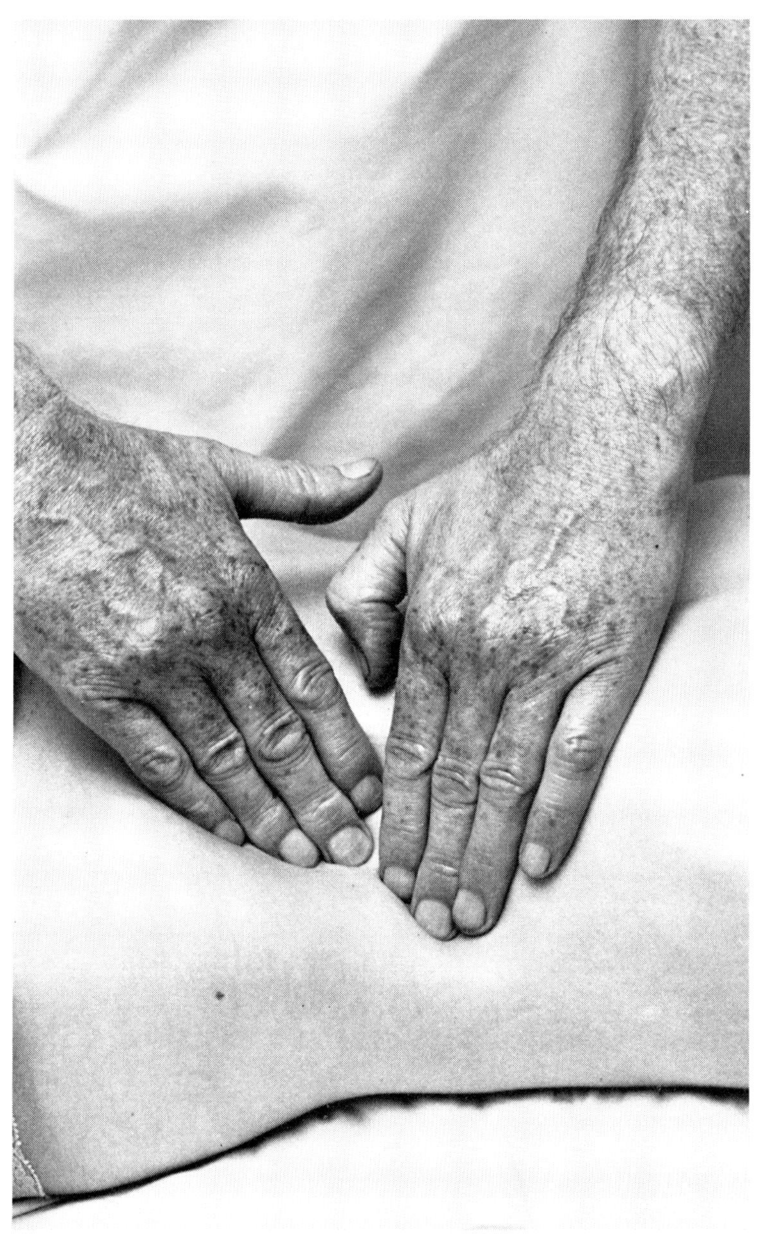

FIG. 21 *Friction to the Descending Colon*

FIG. 22 *Deep Abdominal Massage as an Alternative Using the Forearm*

Massage to the Foot, Leg and Thigh: Posterior Aspect

Return to the right foot, leg and thigh. Apply oil to the foot and leg, then sitting at the end of the right hand side of the plinth with your back turned towards your client, spread a towel on your lap. Now take hold of the foot and apply friction to the base of the phalanges. (See figure number 23.) During the next few minutes, massage the plantar arch, i.e. the underneath area of the foot with the base of your thumb, fingers or fist. Insert your index or third finger in between each of the toes; then flex and extend the toes in your hand as one movement. Finish the foot and ankle with finger pressure to the achilles tendon, at the back of the heel.

The next muscle is the gastrocnemius, that well-presented calf muscle; I appreciate that you have already given it some attention, it is worthy of more. Apply petrissage by picking up and moving your fingers up the full length of this muscle, thus squeezing out the lymph and de-oxygenated blood. Bend the leg until the foot touches the buttocks, or as far as the leg will go without undue stress. (See figure number 24.) Before completely returning the leg to the horizontal position on the touch, hold the leg in the upright position (see figure number 25), and apply a firm effleurage/petrissage to the calf muscle. Your massage, whilst in this position will greatly aid the venous return on its journey to the heart. After applying effleurage from the ankle to the popliteal space (the concave space at the back of the knee), (see figure number 26), return the limb to the rest position on the couch.

Situated at the back of the thigh are the hamstring muscles. They are powerful flexor muscles that flex and rotate the leg. The next sequence is to effleurage and knead, then complete the thigh with effleurage yet again (see figure number 27). These movements are similar to the way that you applied massage to the anterior or front aspect of the thigh. Remember, with practice ease will eventually come. Experiment with your movements bearing always in mind the basic fundamentals of massage. Remember what lies under the skin, and keep a clear picture of what it is that you are trying to effect. It is now time to permutate your movements; try to link different movements together. Upon occasion your client may have extra large thighs; here, if you wish, a little tapotement will be in order. Light cupping and pounding on the thigh muscles should not be amiss. I personally consider that it is unwise to percuss your client at this stage, especially after so much effort to achieve a relaxed condition, however, it is a useful movement at times. Cover and proceed to the left limb. Repeat as above.

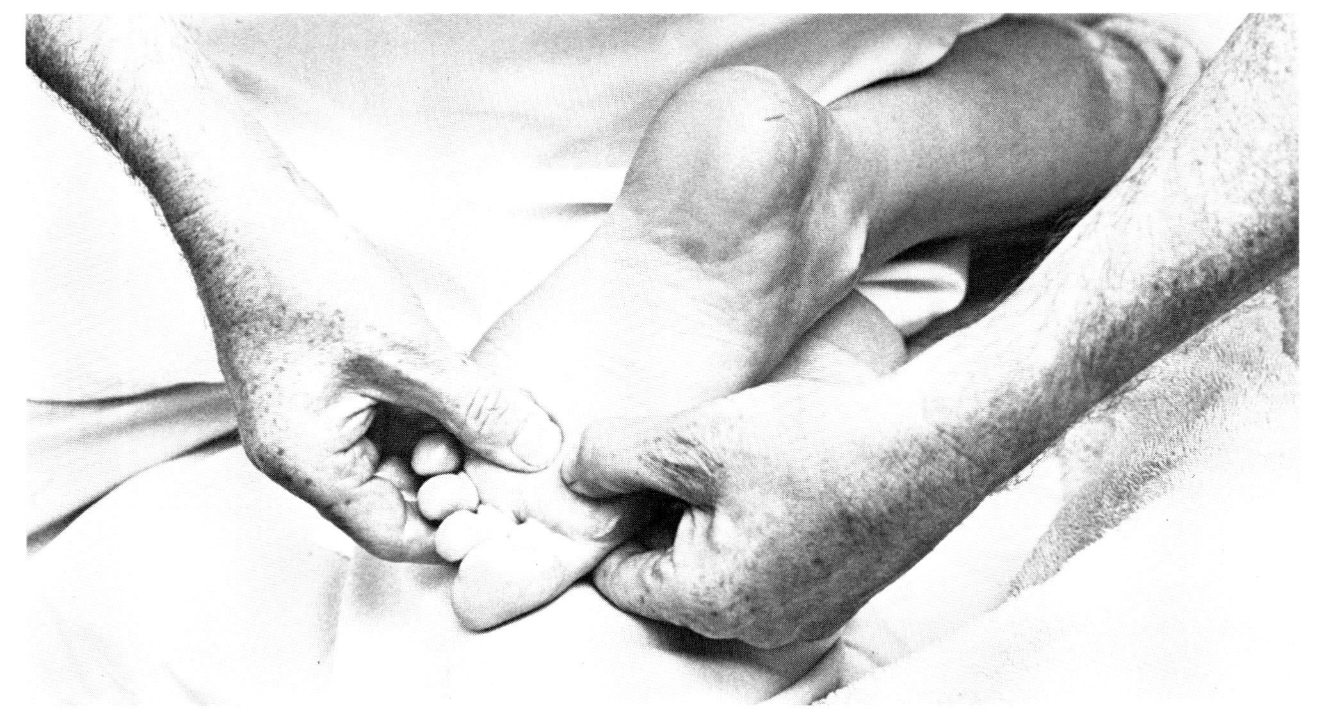

Fig. 23 *Massage to the Base of the Phalanges*

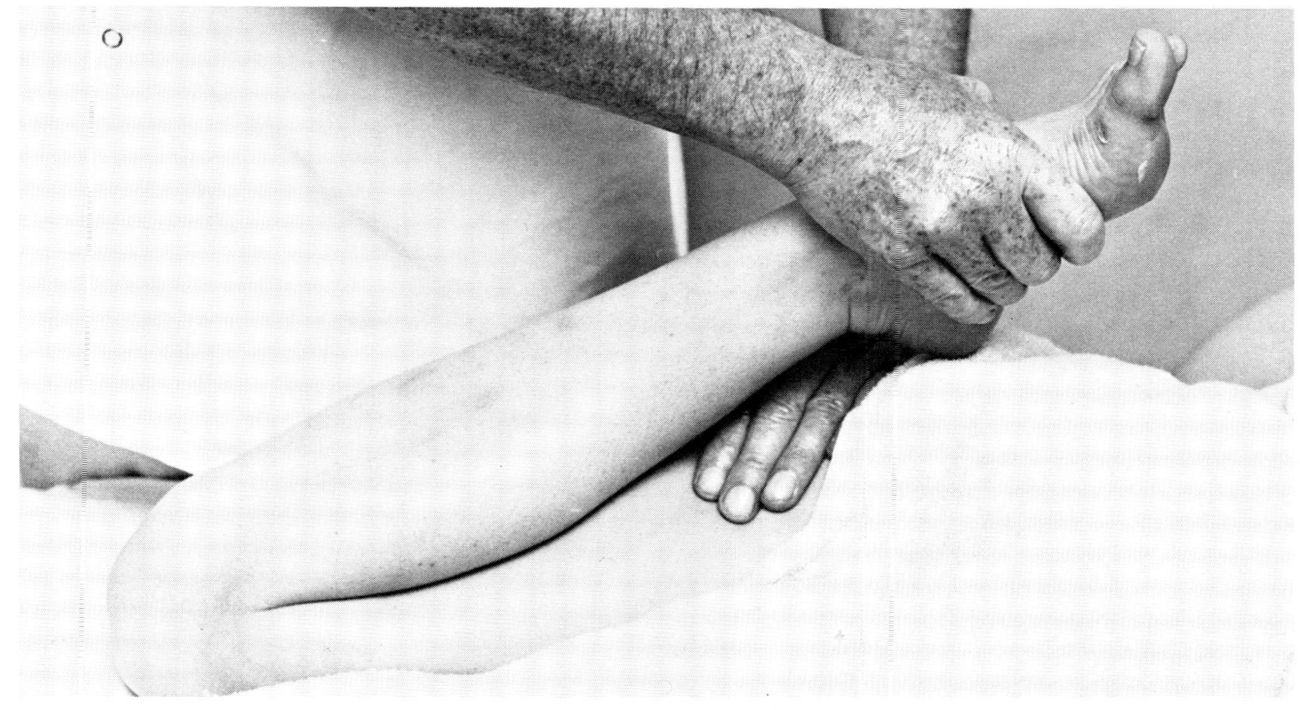

FIG. 24 *Passive Flexion of the Leg*

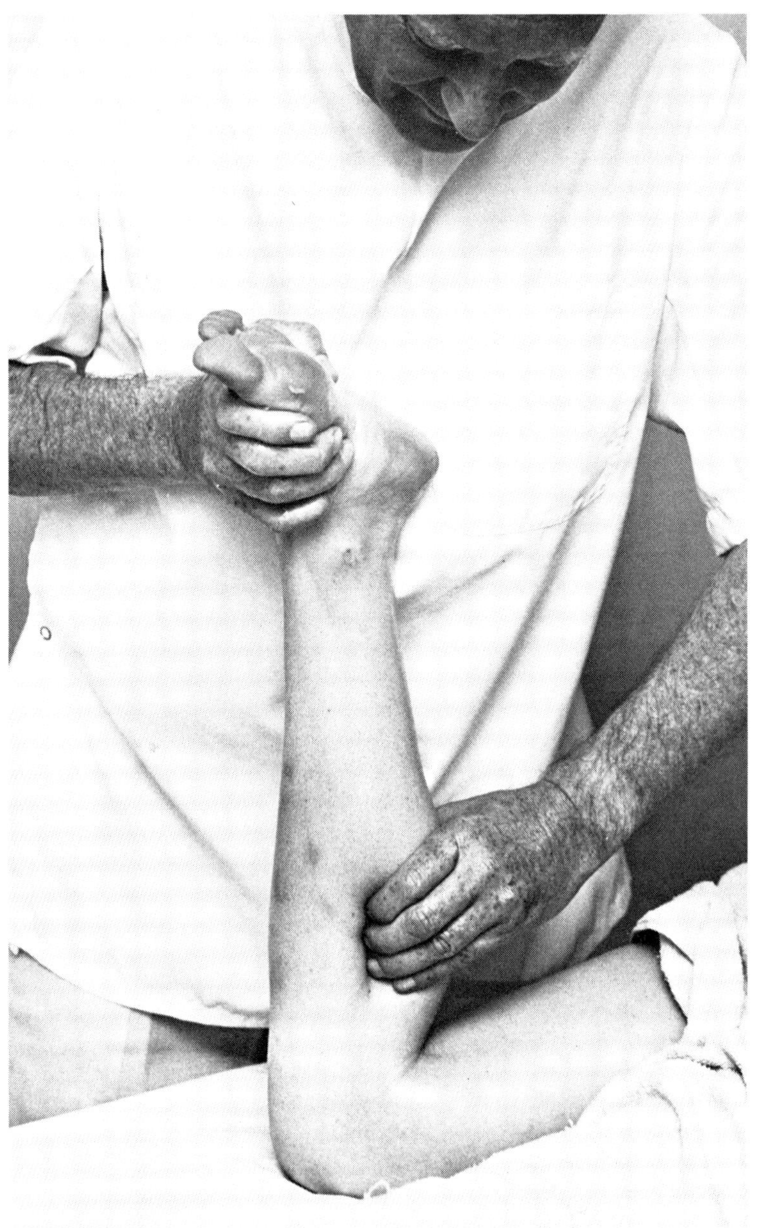

FIG. 25 *Massage to the Calf Muscles with the Body in the Prone Position*

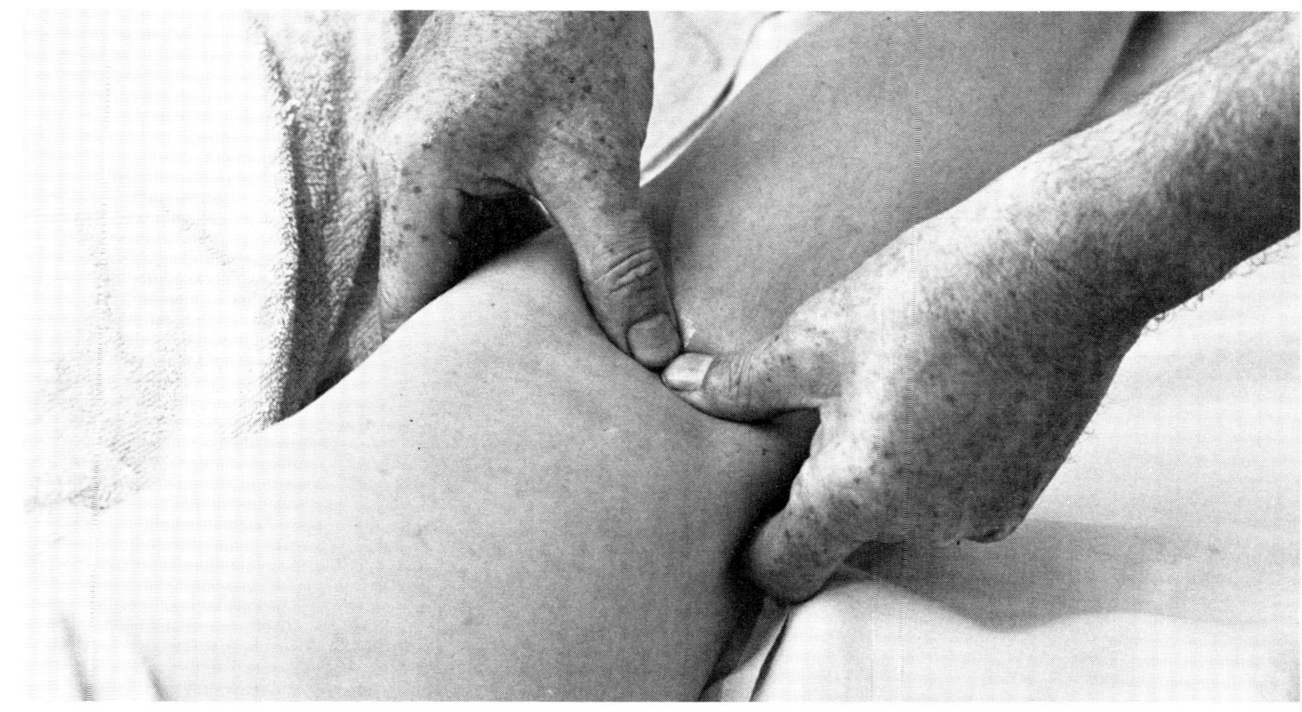

FIG. 26 *Massage to the Popliteal Space at the Back of the Knee*

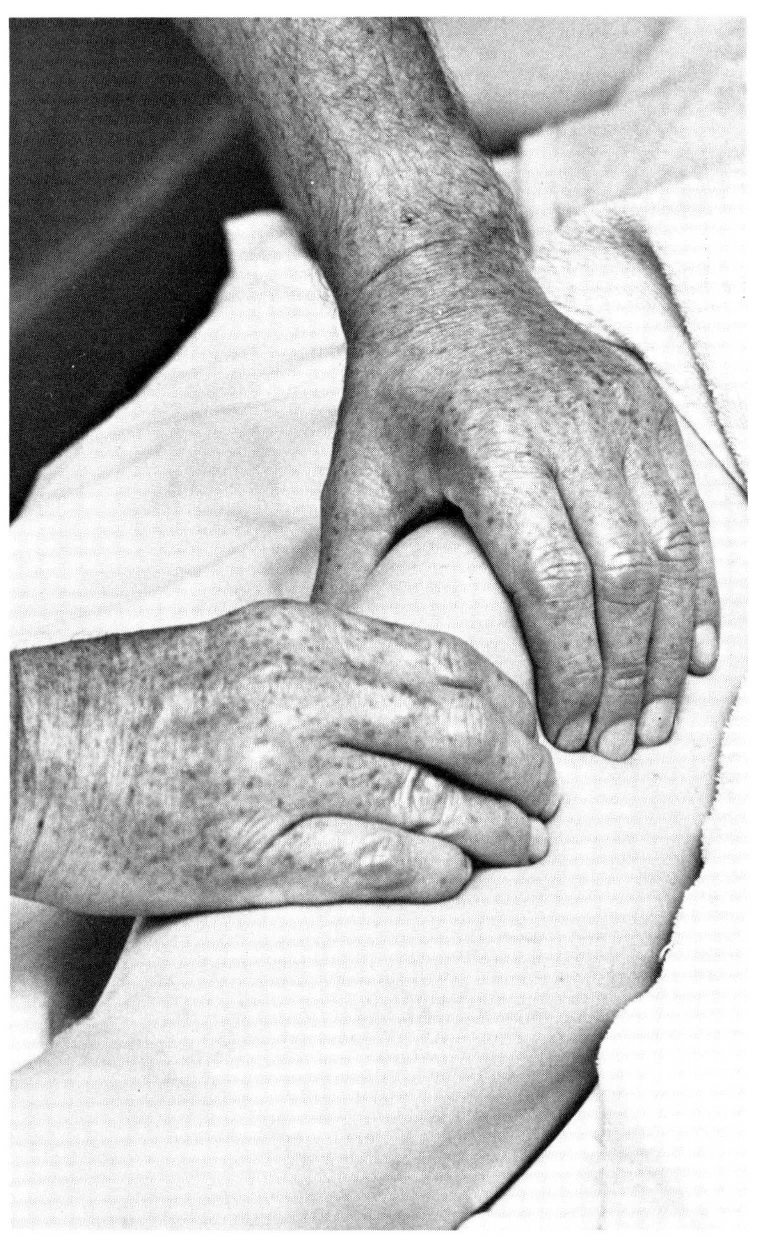

Fig. 27 *Petrissage to the Hamstring Muscles on the Posterior Thigh*

Massage of the Back, Head and Buttocks

The vertebræ that form the centre back of the pelvis, are immovable. Starting with the coccyx at the bottom end of the spine, are four coccygeal vertebræ, adjoined directly by five sacral vertebræ that form the sacrum. On the higher aspect of the pelvis and immediately above, are the lumbar vertebræ. This is where you start massage to the back.

After having completed massage to the lower extremities, i.e. the legs, then proceed to uncover the back until you reach the pelvis, leaving the legs and buttocks completely covered with a towel. Apply oil so as to lubricate the whole of the back. Remember, when applying oil to the body, it is advantageous to spread it completely over the palms of your hands, then place the palmar surface of your hands on to the area about to be massaged. Let your hands follow faithfully the contours of the body, effleurage. This will ensure a maximum transfer of oil in a minimum of time to the person being treated. Still on the left side of the couch, proceed towards the base of the spine.

Place your hands on both sides of the spine, just above the pelvis. Your fingers on the outside and your thumbs touching the spinal processses. These are the protuberances on either side of the spinal column. With a firm pressure traverse the full length of the spine in a slow upward direction, finishing the movement at the nape of the neck. (See figure numbers 28, 29.) Return your hands back to the base of the lumbar spine, keeping them lightly in contact with the body throughout the whole of this movement. On the right and left side are the erector-spinæ muscles; they follow the course of the spine being treated by you now. Start by applying friction with your thumbs to these muscles, on one side of the spine first, then repeat on the opposite side, proceeding in an upward direction. When you reach the scapula, follow the contour of the bottom and inner circumference of the shoulder blade. Make it float under the persuasion of your manipulation until it is pliable. (See figure numbers 30, 31.) Now insert your fingers into this susceptible area; it invites attention. In between the top or leading ridge known as the spine of scapula, and the bottom facet of the shoulder blades, is a slight depression which houses vulnerable pressure points well known in the east. This surface of the scapula would benefit from a little friction if your client enjoys good health; a lot of deep friction should a fibrositic condition exist. However, before treating lesions or pathological conditions, a lot more training will be necessary. This does not mean that you should neglect the shoulder blades. To do so would decrease the value of your massage. Friction and effleurage the whole of this area. Insinuate your fingers into the various depressions; then return to the base of the spine. Clench your fist by holding your hands in the closed position lightly. Extend your hands to make available a row of eight knuckles. Place the knuckles of both hands on the left side of your client's spine, touching the top of the pelvis. Now make a lateral movement applying a little pressure across the surface of the back, finishing the movement lightly on the left side of the body. Return to the left of the spine on the next section of the back, repeating your last movement. Continue with these movements until you reach the neck. Then return again to the position from which you started but this time (still standing on the left side of the couch), place your knuckles on the right side of the spine and repeat the previous movements until you reach the neck. Finish your movement at the neck. You may have noticed that lines have begun to appear across the body. This movement could aptly be called 'the zebra', for reasons that are obvious. (See figure number 32.)

Effleurage the whole of the back. With your hands still in contact with the body, change your position, so that you are now standing in front of your client's head facing the whole of the body. Now apply long movements of effleurage from the shoulders to the buttocks. Continue with a zebra movement on each side of the spine. Traverse the whole length of the vertebræ in a downward movement. Return to the neck; zebra this time by spacing your hands further apart and traverse the full length of the back again. (See figure numbers 33 and 34.) Return once more to the neck. With your hands placed flat upon the back, one on either side, let your fingers gather the skin rolling it inwards and downwards. Concentrate on the susceptible shoulders that benefit so much from massage, then complete the rest of the back with similar movements. This is probably one of the few times that it is permissible to massage away from the heart. Return to the left hand side of the couch and with your hands resting on either side of the upper spine, apply a light-sharp-pressure. It is particularly beneficial to smokers as it helps to empty the lungs of any stale cigarette smoke that may have accumulated. A little kneading to the waist now would be beneficial. (See figure number 36), then uncover the buttocks; apply oil and effleurage. There is far too much muscle here for you to miss. The gluteal muscles respond favourably to pressure; however, direct all of your movements towards the centre, which is the gluteal fold. (See figure numbers 37 and 38.) Later, with experience you will locate the insertion of the sciatic nerve which will enable you to help people suffering from sciatica as well as other disorders of the thighs and legs. At present be content to massage, try to co-ordinate your movements until a smooth lucidity ensues from the vital quality of your massage.

A note here about head and scalp massage. I nearly always give a digital vibratory massage to the scalp. (See figure number 39.) Of course I have the good sense to leave well alone, especially if the client is female and has spent some hours at the hairdressers. What wonderful attention our hair gets! Start by standing at the top left side of the couch, and after cleansing your hands with alcohol, place your fingers on either side of your client's forehead at rest on the scalp, then WILL them to vibrate. This movement comes from the very centre of your being. It will be necessary to practice this often. Move from the front towards the back of the head, manipulating the whole of the area. Return to the crown, replacing your hands on either side of the head, this time gather up the loose scalp, causing it to move over the skull freely. If you can manage these two movements, circulation to the scalp will improve.

Remaining on the left side of the couch, have some alcohol available and pour a small quantity on to your hands, spreading it immediately on your client's back. This is a technique used in hot countries and I find it useful here. Allow the leading edge of your hands to tap lightly upon your client's back in quick succession. Keep the palmar surface of your hands as close as you can together throughout this movement. When you can percuss your client's back lightly and with a little speed, it will become an exhilarating experience. This movement is known as hacking (see figure number 40). Now change to pounding and with your fist lightly clenched, pound the shoulders (see figure number 41). In fact you may percuss most of the back, carefully avoiding the kidneys which are situated on either side of the body in the small of the back. Alternate with both of your hands remembering to keep the pounding light. Should you find this difficult, do not be concerned as it is not essential to give tapotement in order to give a good massage. Tapotement however, is good as a stimulant bringing blood to the surface muscles and to the sensory nerves that are contained in the epidermis. Now 'cup' your hands letting them fall in quick succession upon your client's back. (See figure number 42.) If your hands are insufficiently cupped, there will be no cushion of air to absorb the direct contact and the movement will become slapping and painful. So do take heed and do not become over enthusiastic; enjoy the movements. Sometimes at this point I take a towel and holding it loosely in both of my hands, try to do a combination of friction coupled with plain rubbing through the fabric. This ensures the removal of most of the unabsorbed oil as well as conveying a good feeling to the client. Discard the towel and lightly effleurage the back, then apply petrissage to the superior surface of the trapezius on both sides of the body. These muscles will respond to this stimuli par-excellence. (See figure number 35.) Effleurage once more the whole of the back lightly and without rushing. With two or three fingers of one hand, slowly, sensitively and yet hardly touching the back, traverse the full spinal vertebræ from the lumbar area to the base of the skull, finishing your massage at the neck. Now cover and allow your client a short rest.

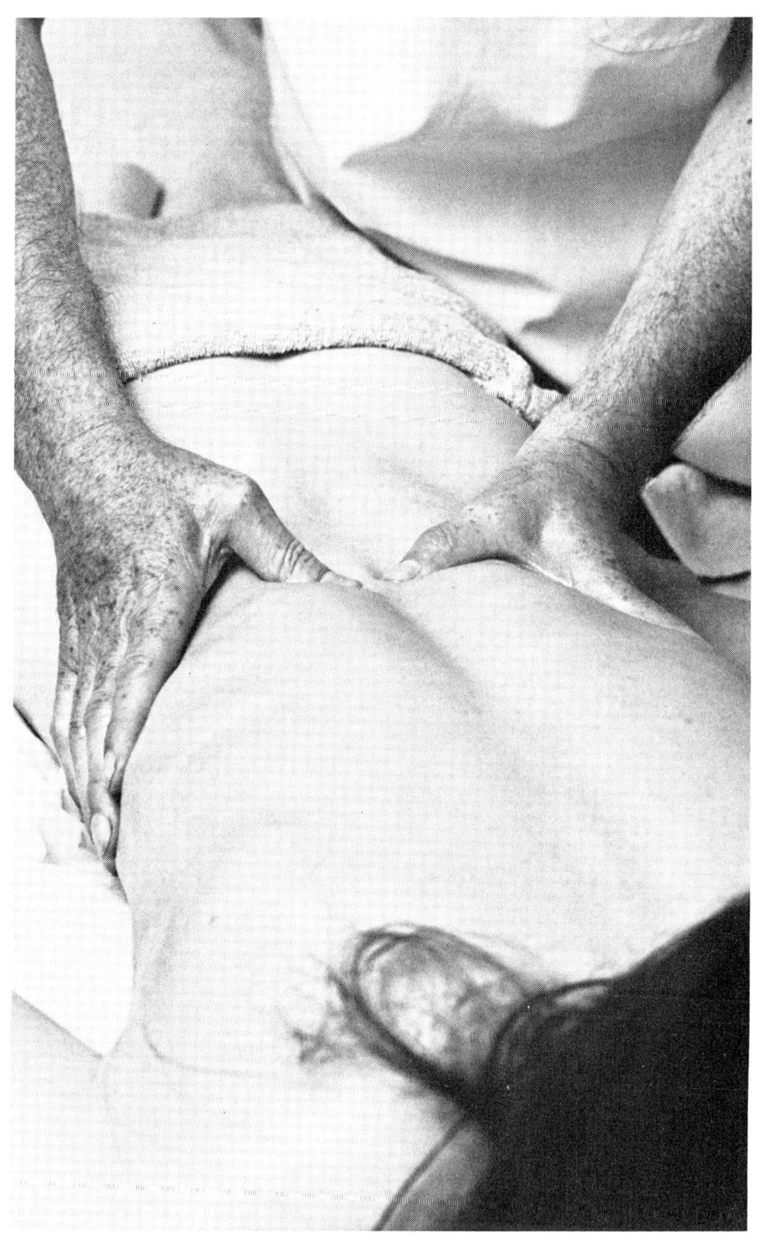

Fig. 28 *Manipulating the Spinal Vertebræ, 1st Movement*

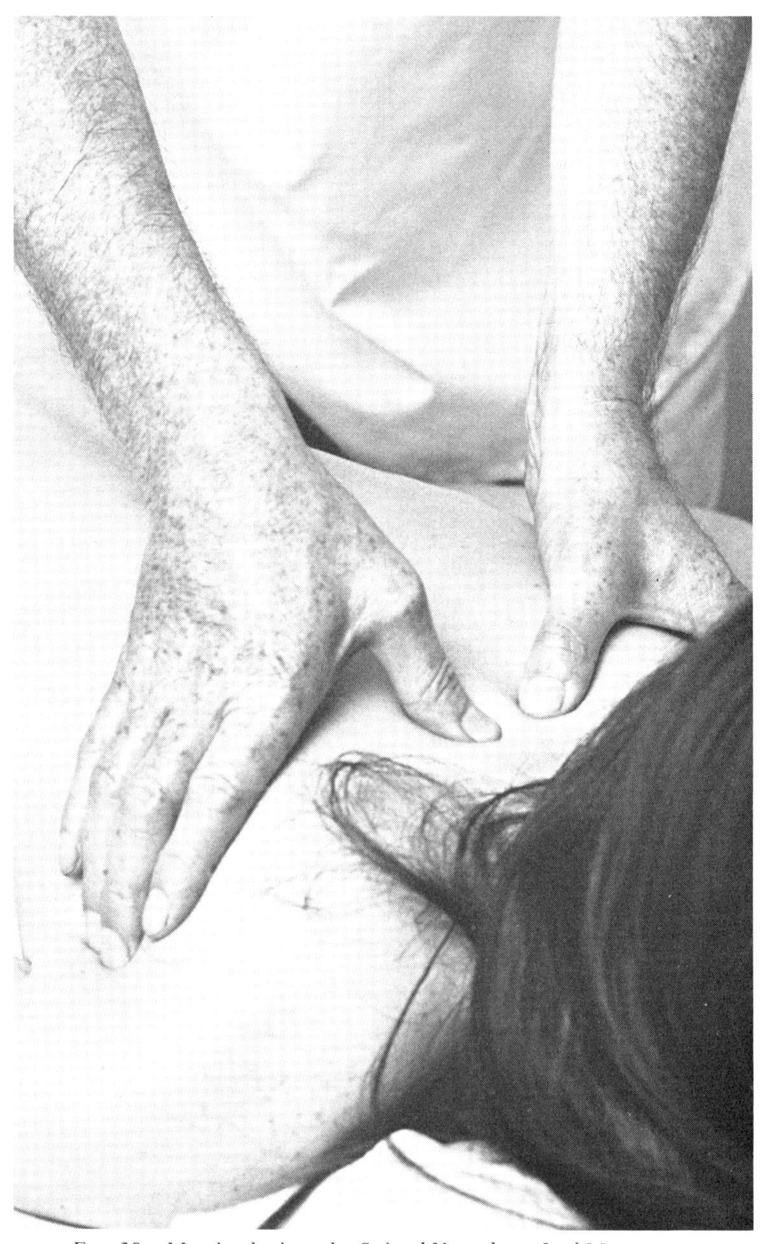

FIG. 29 *Manipulating the Spinal Vertebræ, 2nd Movement*

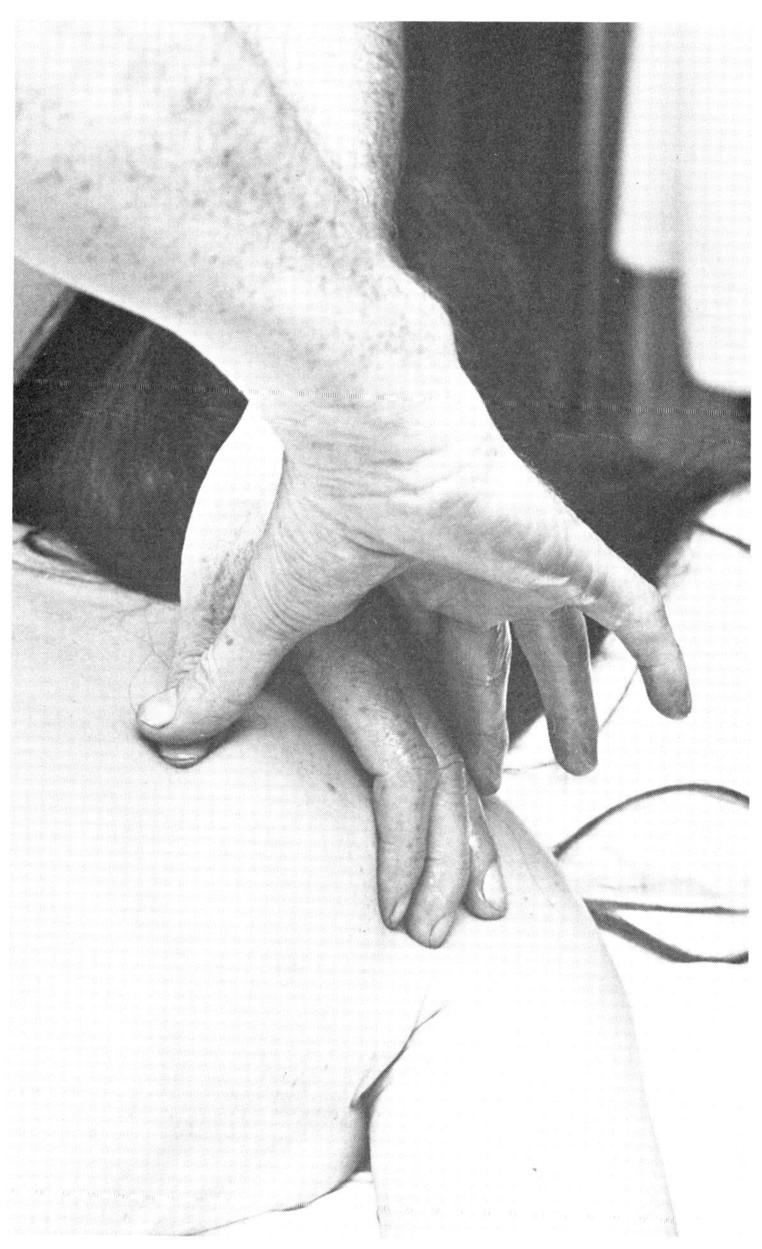

FIG. 30 *Circumscribing the Scapula with the Thumb Buttressed for Extra Strength*

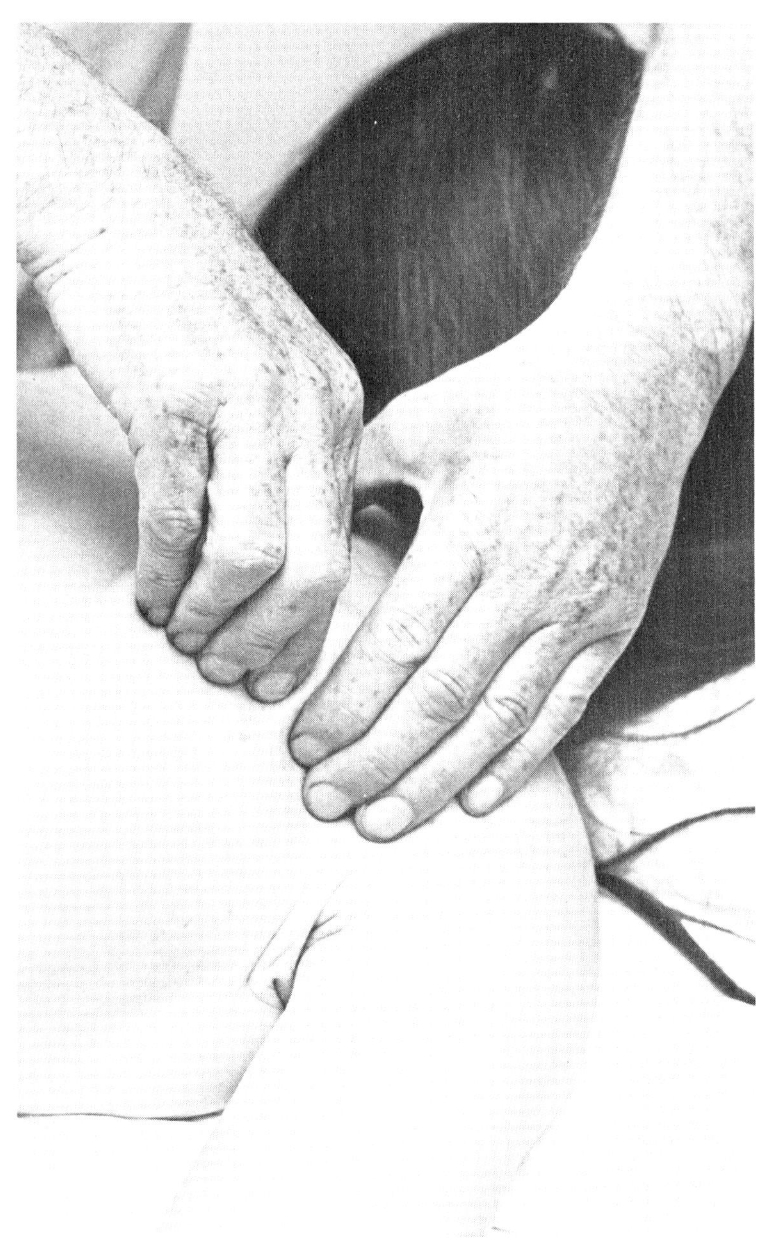

Fig. 31 *Circumscribing the Scapula*

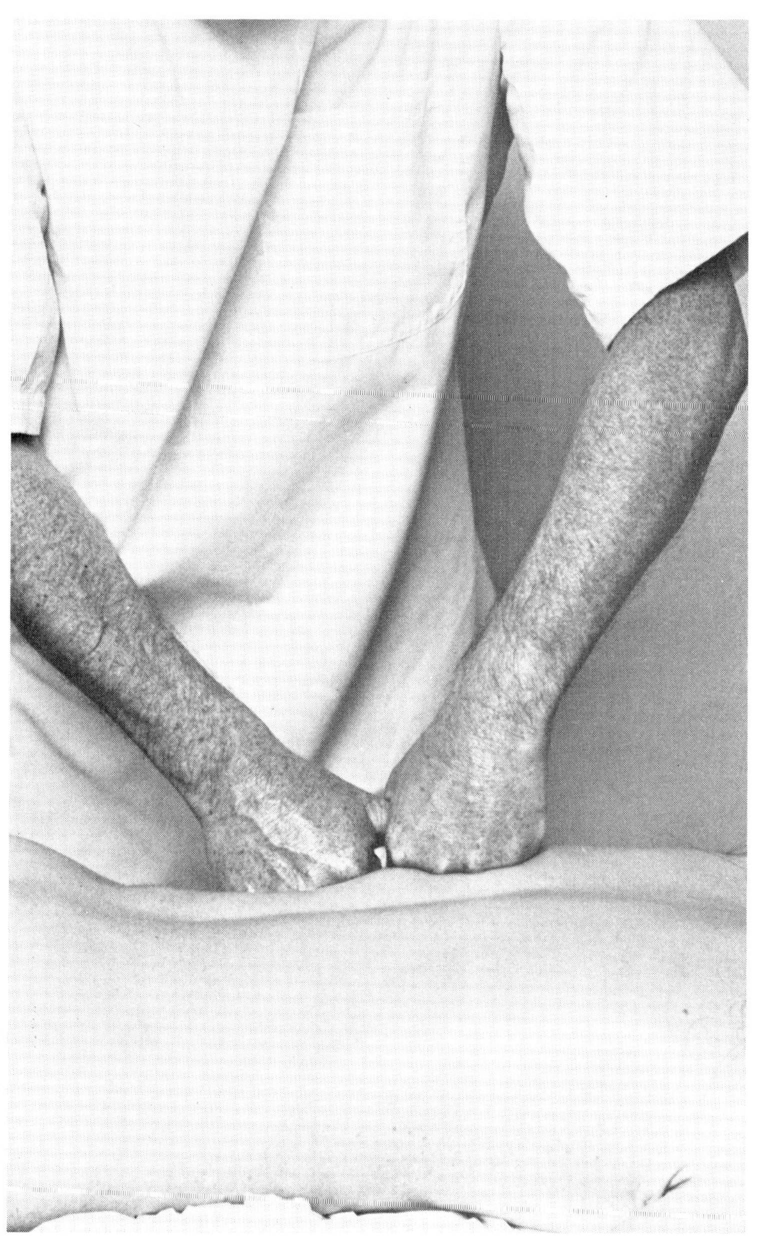

FIG. 32 *Zebra Movement to the Left Side of the Spine*

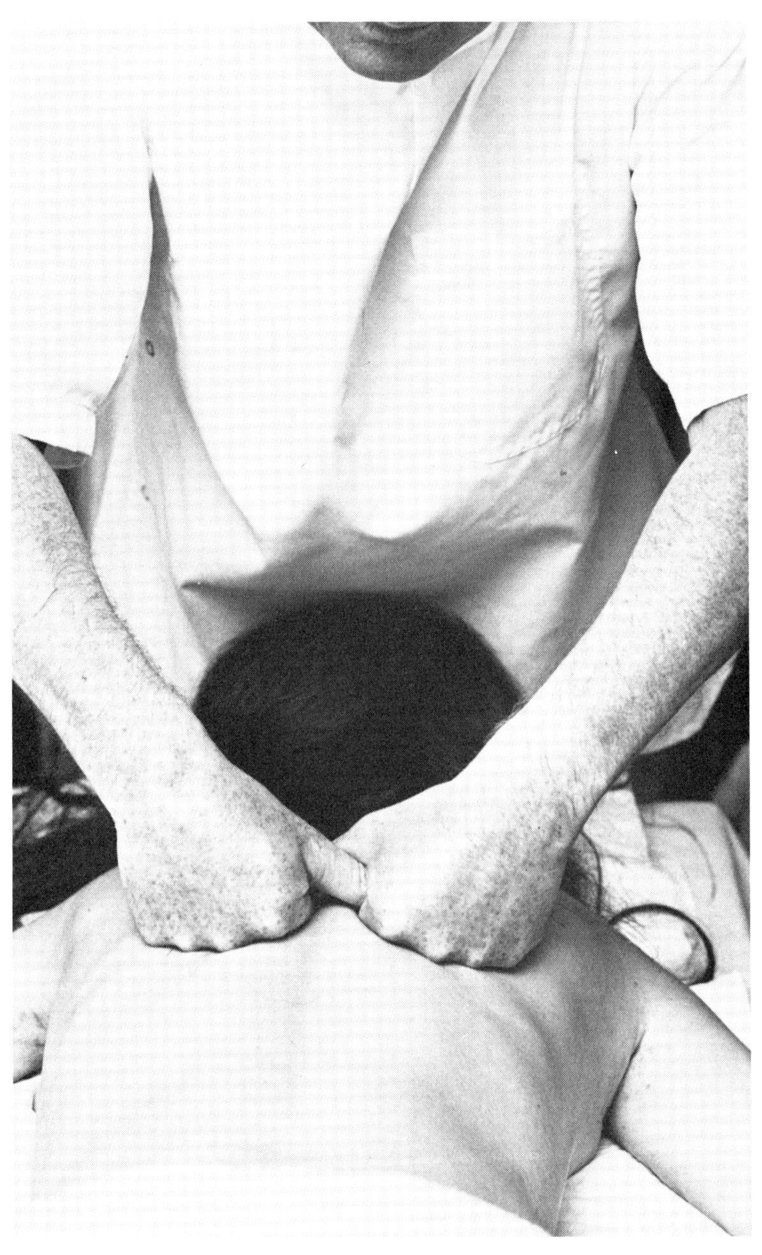

FIG. 33 *Zebra Movement Traversing the Spine*

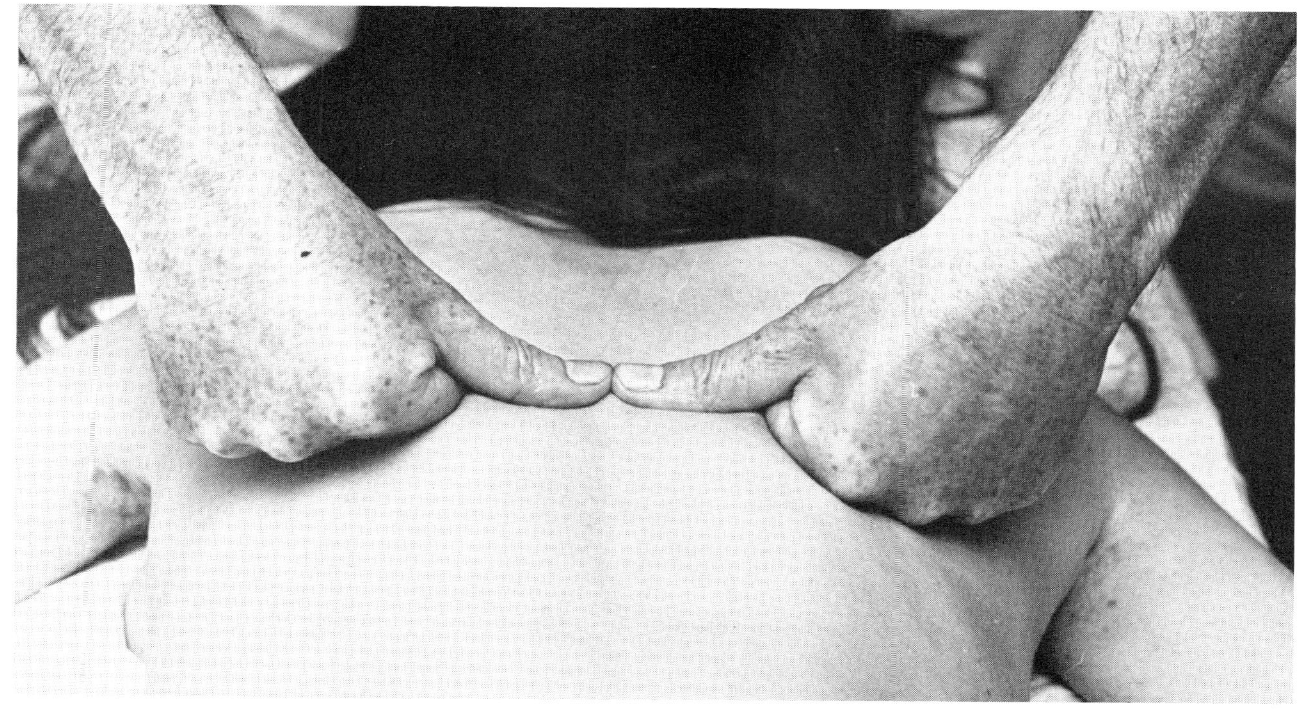

Fig. 34 *Zebra Movement with the Thumbs Acting as a Gauge*

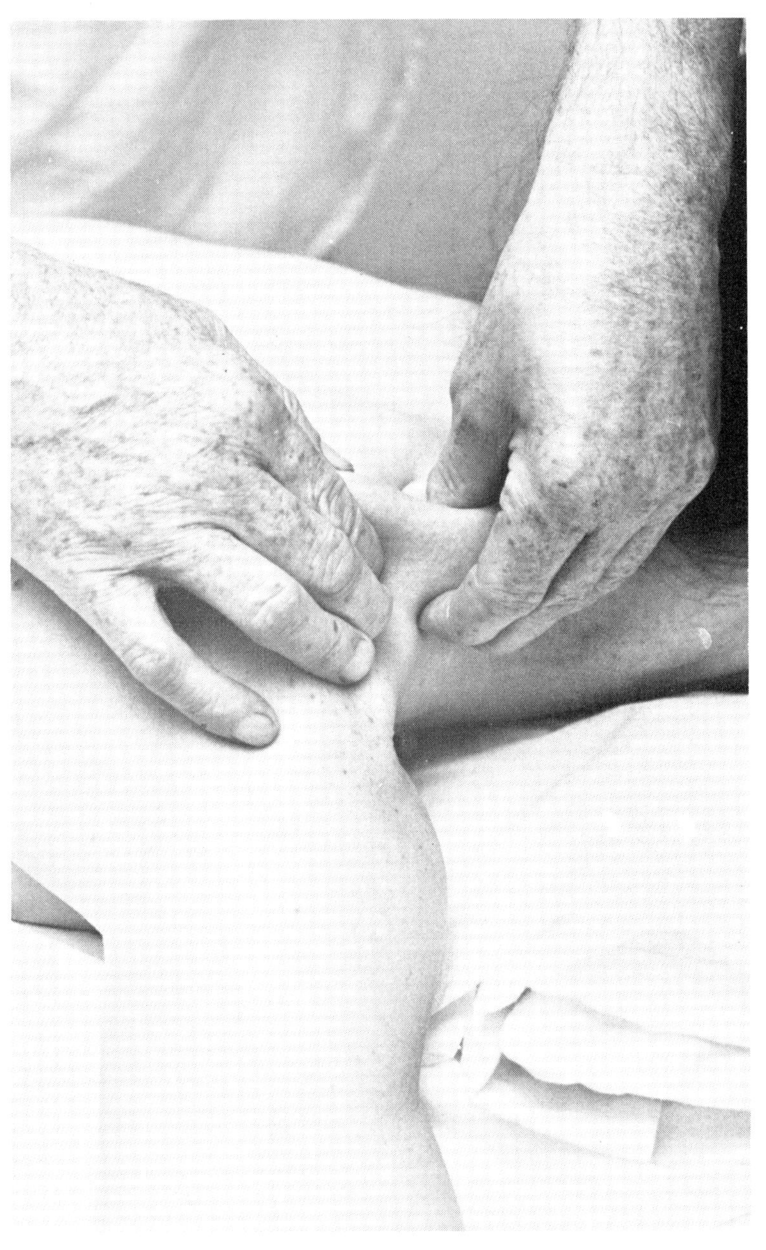

FIG. 35 *Petrissage to the Trapezius*

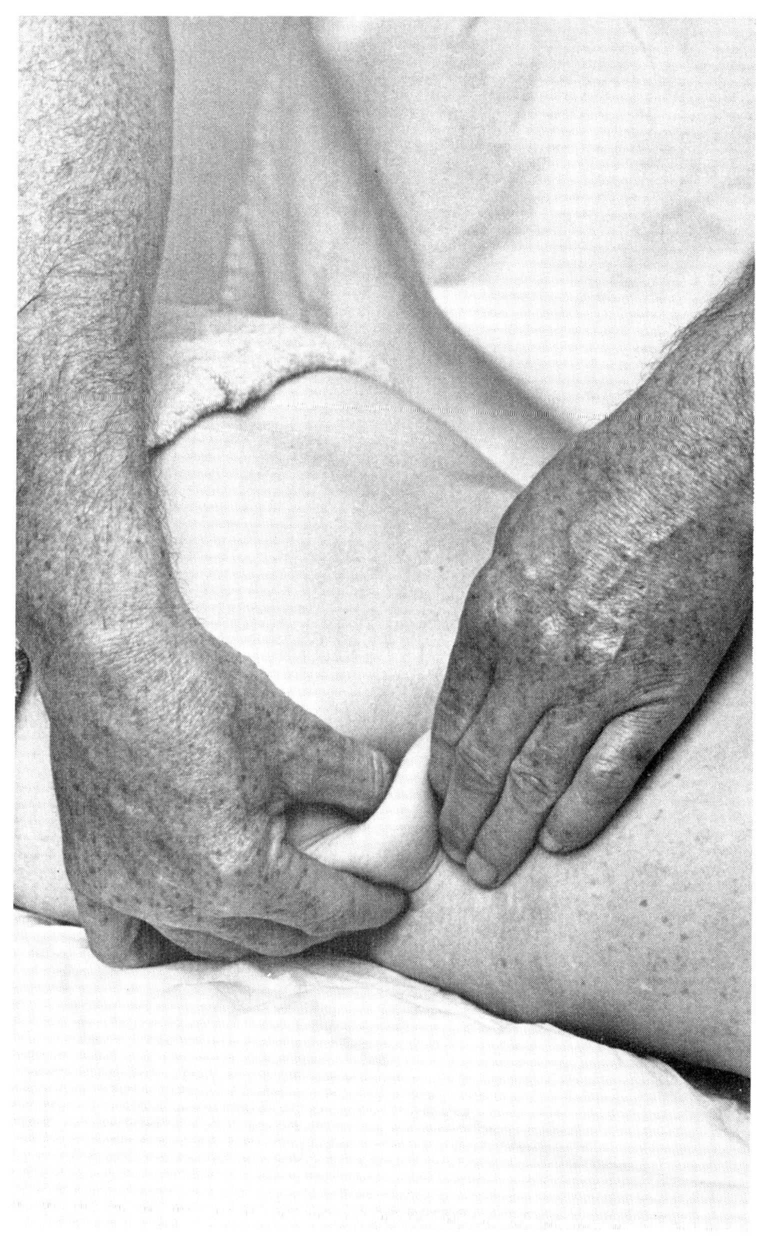

FIG. 36 *Kneading to the Waist*

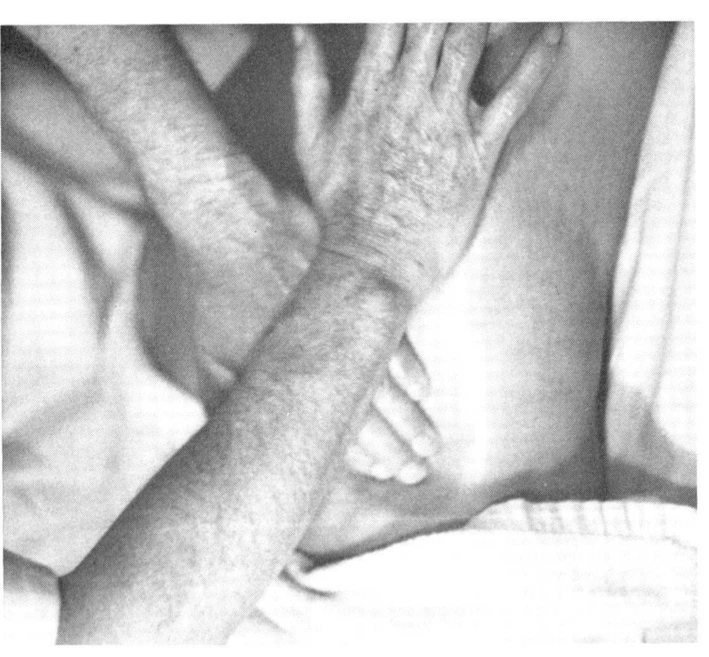

Fig. 37 *Kneading the Buttocks with the Flat of the Hands*

Fig. 38 *Kneading the Buttocks with the Fist*

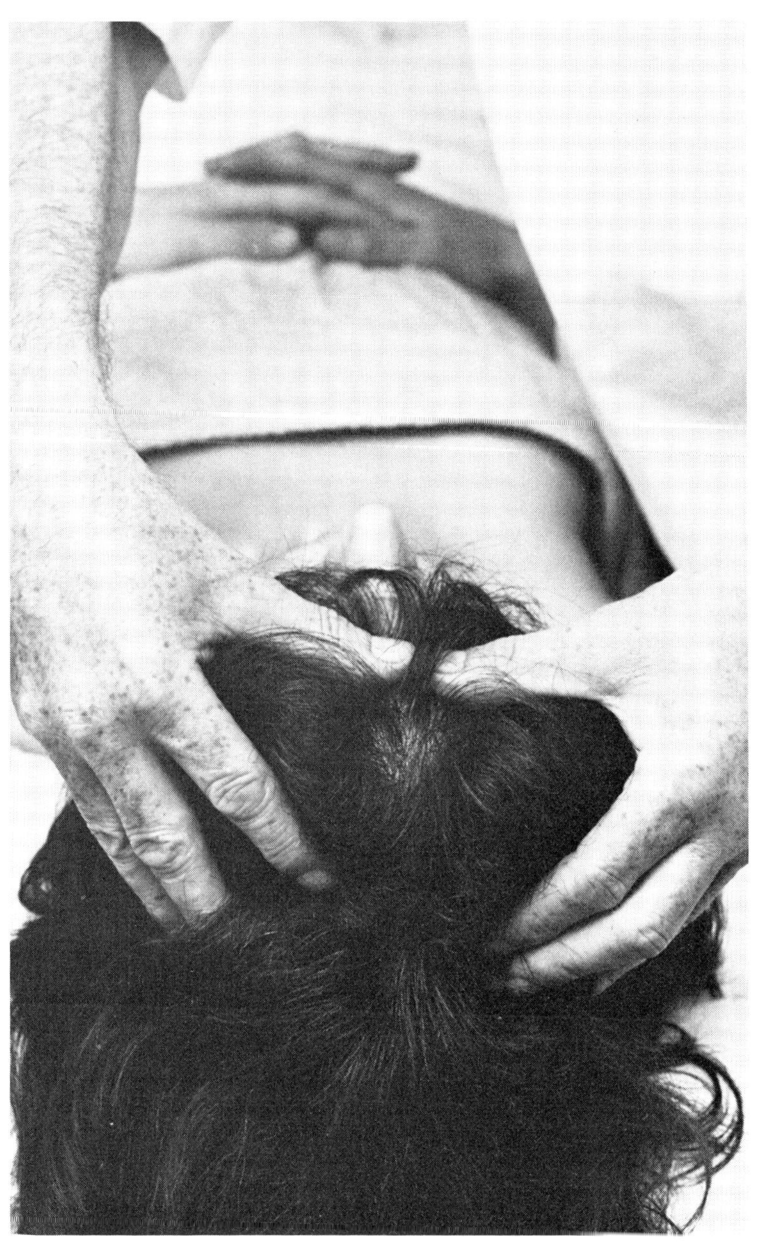

FIG. 39 *Digital Vibration to the Head and Scalp*

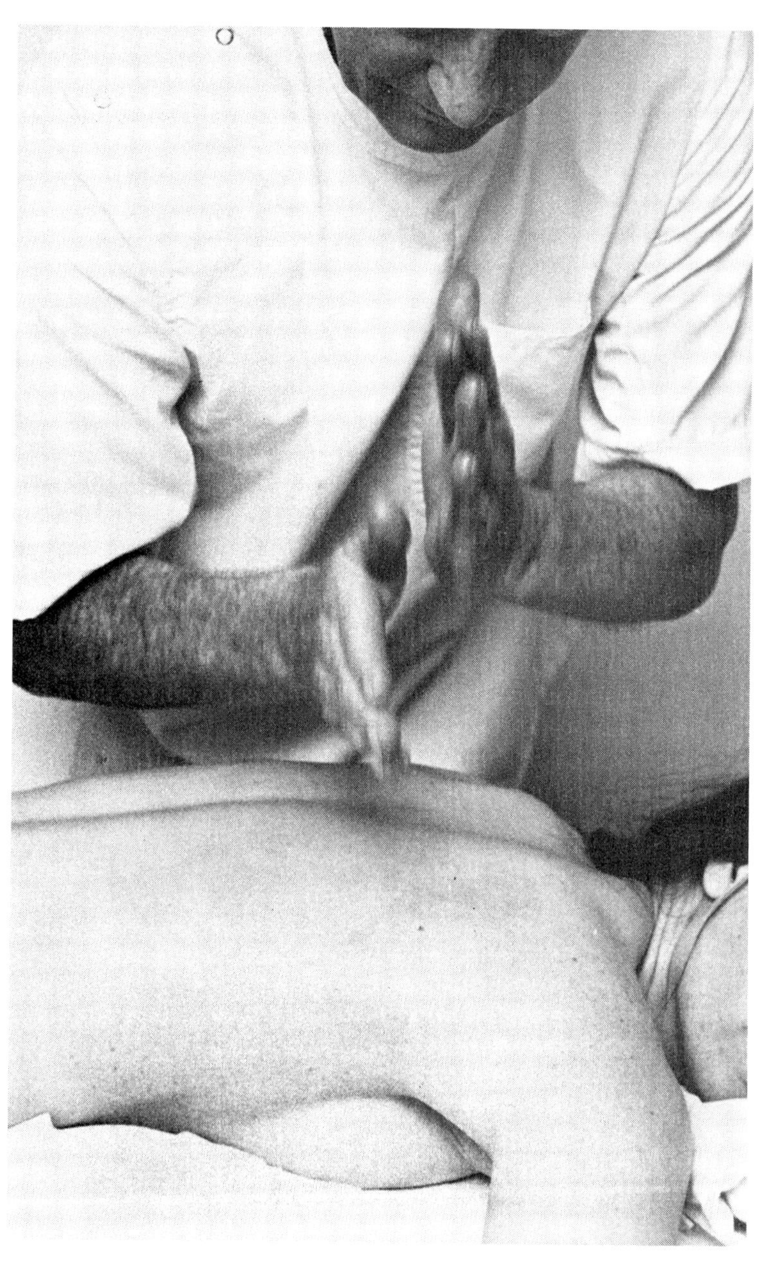

FIG. 40 *Tapotement: Hacking*

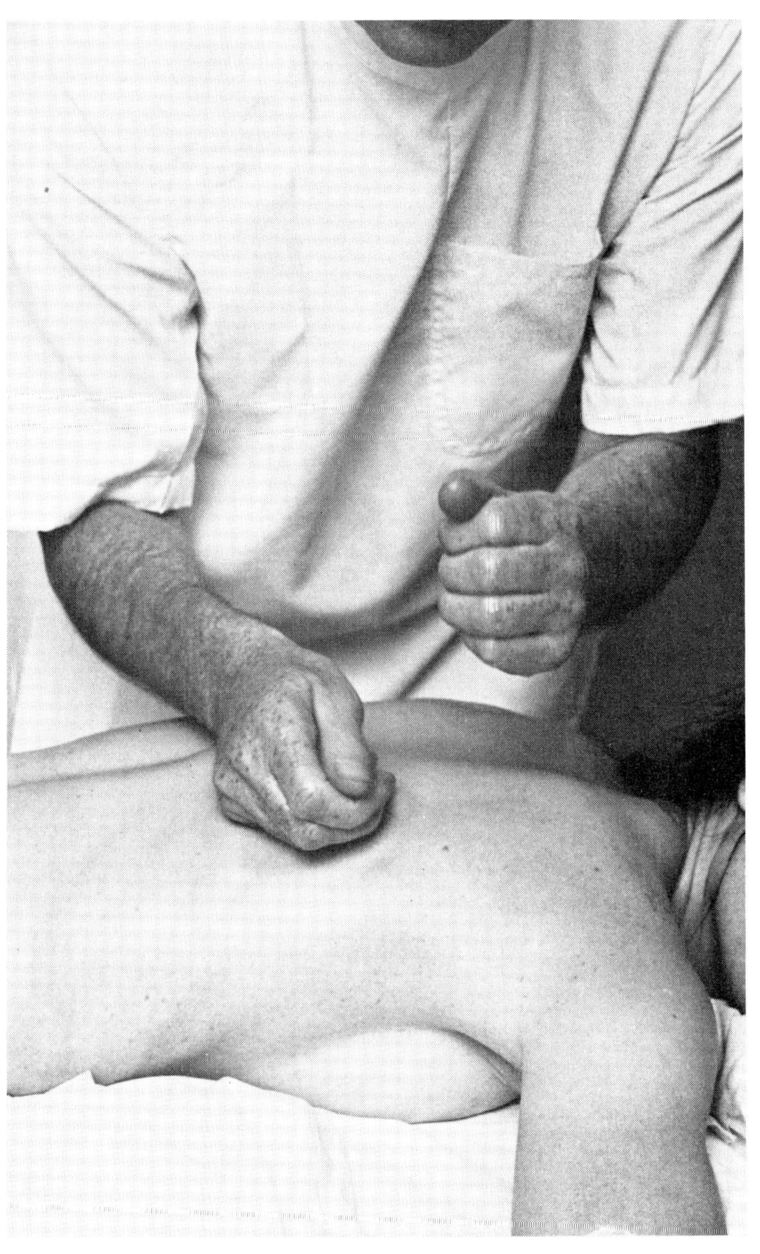

FIG. 41 *Tapotement: Pounding the Scapula*

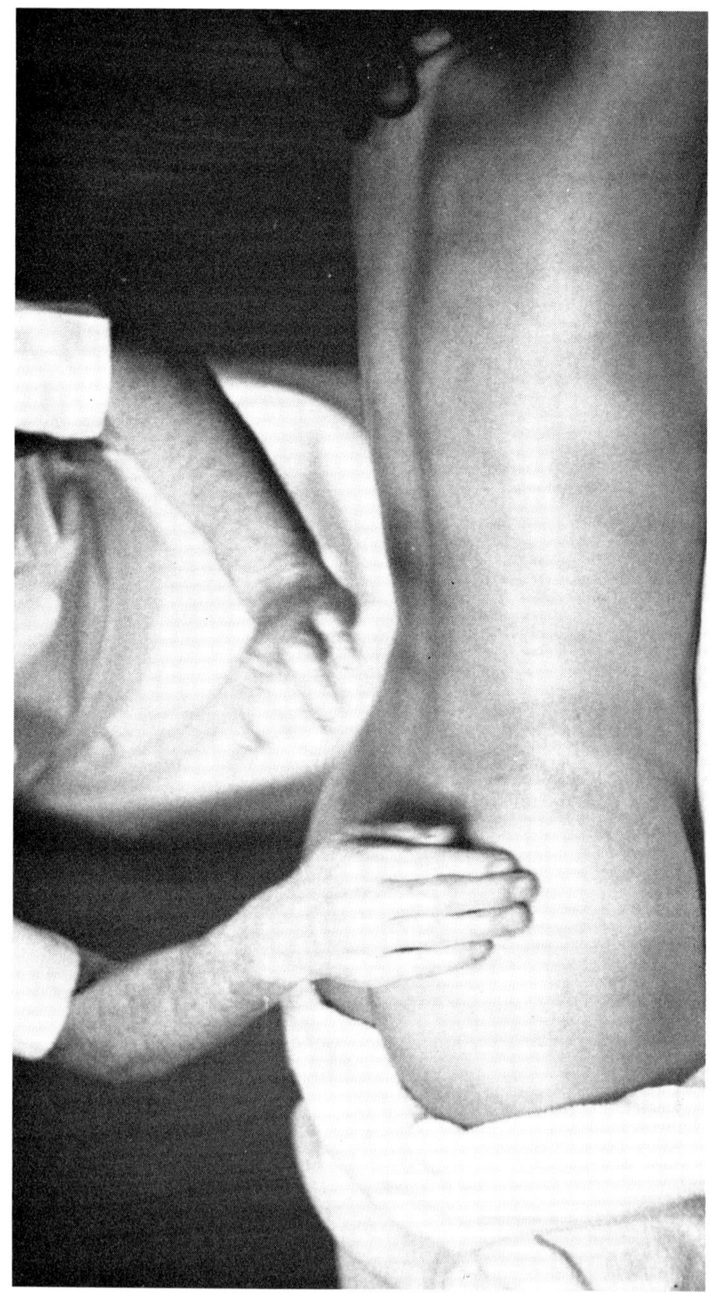

FIG. 42 *Tapotement: Cupping*

Massage Procedure Condensed

SUPINE POSITION; YOUR CLIENT LYING ON HIS BACK

1 Manipulate the fingers and the back surface of the left hand.
2 Knead the muscles of the palm.
3 Flex and extend the wrist
4 Effleurage to the forearm.
5 Effleurage and petrissage to the biceps, the triceps and the deltoid.
Cover with a towel.

Proceed to the left foot

1 Hold the left foot firmly and effleurage.
2 Manipulate the toes and the metatarsals.
3 Massage the toes with the palmar surface of both hands, using the mount at the base of the thumbs.
4 Effleurage the foot including the achilles tendon.
5 Assert a pressure movement to the plantar arch (underneath the foot).

Proceed to the leg

1 Oil and effleurage from the ankle to the knee.
2 Raise the leg and knead the calf muscle with both hands.
3 Effleurage.

Proceed to the knee

1 Circumscribe the patella (the knee cap) with your fingers and thumbs several times.
2 Palpate so as to ensure movement.

Proceed to the thigh

1 Apply oil and effleurage to the whole of the thigh.

2 Knead the full length of the vastus externus (the muscle on the outer side of the thigh).
3 Knead the sartorius
4 Knead the quadriceps extensors.
5 Effleurage.

Continuing around the body in a clockwise direction

Proceed to the right leg: repeat

Proceed to the right arm: repeat

Proceed to the neck

1 Oil and hand-roll the posterior neck muscles about three times.
2 Back of the head position, insert hands under the shoulder blades with the fingers towards and touching the upper dorsal and lower cervical spinal processes. Withdraw your hands completely as far as the nape of the neck, at the same time giving a gentle lift of the neck and head. Repeat three times.

Return to the upper left side of the body

1 Friction to both sides of the posterior neck (optional).
2 Insinuate your fingers into the superior and inferior clavical recesses. (The space above and under the collar bone), giving a gentle manipulation.
3 Knead the upper pectorals.

Men only

1 Effleurage the whole of the chest with bold sweeping movements.

Proceed to the abdomen

1 Raise and support the knees, gently oil the abdomen.
2 Effleurage in a clockwise direction.
3 Apply friction to the ascending, transverse and descending colon.
4 Effleurage.

Proceed to your client's right leg

1 Sit on the edge of the couch and place the right foot in your lap. Effleurage and apply pressure to the plantar arch. (Underneath the foot.)
2 Friction to the arch and run your fingers in between the toes.
3 Massage the heel and the achilles tendon.

Proceed to the leg

1 Further oil to the gastrocnemius (calf muscle).
2 Petrissage from the heel to the popliteal space at the back of the knee.
3 Bend the leg to a 90° angle and effleurage.
Replace leg on to the couch.

Proceed to the thigh

1 Oil the posterior thigh.
2 Effleurage to the hamstrings and knead these muscles similar to the anterior thigh.
3 Effleurage and cover.

Proceed to the left leg: repeat

Position on the left side of the couch

1 Apply oil to the whole of the back.
2 Manipulate the spine with your thumbs on either side of the spinal processes.
3 Apply friction to the left and right erector spinæ muscles on either side of the spine.
4 Manipulate and massage the right and left shoulder blades.
5 Zebra to the left and right of the spine.
6 Knead the waist muscles.
7 Effleurage.

Position at the head of the couch facing the feet

1 Effleurage the whole of the back and knead the shoulders.
2 Zebra movement the whole length of the spine.
3 Zebra movement with your thumbs acting as a gauge.
4 Gather the skin from the left and the right side of the body.
5 Effleurage.

Return to the left side of the couch

1 Further massage to the back; effleurage, knead and apply friction.
2 Give a downward pressure over the spine and scapulæ avoiding the area of the kidneys.
3 Effleurage.

Uncover the buttocks

1 Apply oil with the flat of the hands.
2 Knead well and cover.

Cleanse your hands of all oil before proceeding to the head

1 Start at the top of the skull and working towards the neck, try and effect an intuitive-digital-vibro massage.
2 For men, loosen the scalp generally.

Return to the back

1 Effleurage.
2 Percuss with hacking, pounding and cupping.
3 Effleurage.
4 Friction through a towel.
5 Your signing off stroke.
Cover.

Conclusion

Colour, Sound and Touch are all sensory stimulants essential to life's experience. We are bound by physical laws, which are interpreted by personal perception through our data-bank. Sometimes we violate these laws which results in disease. Drug therapy can, upon occasion be very helpful and to many the only acceptable method of healing. The point that should be understood, is that you cannot correct a dislocated inter-vertebral-disc by simply taking a tablet. The pain removed, the cause remains to give more discomfort when the effect of the drug wears off. Sometimes when healing takes effect in the absence of orthodox medicine, the word 'coincidence' comes into its own. People who use this word to explain everything, cannot clearly define their chosen expression. What a coincidence!

Whether or not to heal is rather like saying: to do good or not to do good. One's own conscience, ability, gifts, must be the deciding factors: to each his own. 'Do-Gooders', do not always do good.

Should you, the reader, have gleaned a little more understanding about the human frame and its functions, as well as methods to help, then this introductory book will have served its purpose. My wish is for you to succeed with your efforts. Never allow yourself to forget that the person being massaged entrusts to you his body: a highly complicated, intricate machine. Enjoy your work, pleasure is a recreation. Pass on your good feelings to your client; let empathy reign supreme.

Should you now feel that this is indeed just the beginning, then I suggest that you enrol with an institute. For those of you who wish not to proceed further, you have the satisfaction of being enriched by the knowledge of your new found art.

GOOD LUCK.

Glossary

GENERAL

Anatripsis Rubbing up
Anterior Front Aspect
Arteries Main blood Vessels
Auricle An upper Chamber of the Heart
Capillaries A miniscule Network of Blood Vessels supplying Blood to the Cells
Coccyx The four Coccygeal Vertebræ that form the lower end of the Spine
Cervical Vertebræ The seven Vertebræ situated in the Neck
Clavicle The Collar Bone
Colon The ascending, transverse and descending Colon are all part of the large Intestine.
Distal Furthest end from the Heart.
Dorsal Vertebræ Vertebræ of the upper Back
Extensors Muscles that extend a Limb
Erector Spinæ A Muscle that lies on each side of the Spinal-Vertebral-Column
Erythrocytes Red Corpuscles
Effleurage A stroking movement of Massage
Epigastric An area of the Abdomen
Flexors Muscles that flex a Limb
Friction A Movement of Massage
Gluteal The Gluteus Maximus, Medius and Minimus Muscles of the Buttocks
Hacking A Percussion Movement of Massage
Hypochondriac An Area of the Abdomen
Hypogastric As above
Intercostal Muscles Muscles Situated in between the Ribs
Iliac An Area of the Abdomen
Lumbar Vertebræ Vertebræ in the Lower Back
Latissimus Dorsi A Major Muscle of the Back
Lymphatic Appertaining to the Lymphatic System
Leucocytes White Corpuscles
Lymph Stale De-Oxygenated Blood
Lymphatic Duct A Lymph Duct
Masseur (pronounced Mas-ser) A Male who practises Massage
Masseuse (pronounced Mas-sers) A Female Who Practises Massage
Osmosis Absorption of Liquid through Tissue
Posterior The Back Aspect

Proximal The End nearest to the Heart
Pelvis A bowl-shaped Bone Structure that encases Viscera of the Lower Abdomen
Plinth A Massage Couch
Pectoralis Major A Muscle situated in the Upper Chest
Petrissage A Kneading Movement of Massage
Prone Lying on one's Front
Pancreas An Organ of the Body that aids the Digestion
Peristalsis A Muscular Action of Undulating Ripples
Pounding A Percussion Movement of Massage
Rectus Abdominus A Large Muscle of the Abdomen
Sacrum Is comprised of five Sacral Vertebræ situated in the upper centre of the Pelvis
Scapula Shoulder Blade
Scapulæ Plural to the above
Sternum The Breast Bone
Sterno-Cleido-Mastoideus A Muscle of the Neck
Supinate To turn towards the Front
Supine Lying on one's Back
Spinal Protuberances These are to be found Protruding on either side of the Spinal Vertebræ. They extend from each Vertebra
Trapezius A Muscle that covers the Shoulders and the Back in the Shape of a Trapezium
Thoracic Duct A Lymphatic Duct
Tapotement Any Percussion Movement of Massage
Umbilical An Abdominal Area
Vascular System The Circulatory System
Veins Vessels that Return the Blood to the Heart
Ventrical A lower Chamber of the Heart
Venæ Cavæ Superior and Inferior, Veins that return the Blood directly into the Heart

ANATOMICAL REFERENCES OF THE UPPER EXTREMITIES

Annular Ligament A cartilaginous Band that gives Support to the Wrist
Biceps A twin-headed flexor Muscle of the Arm
Carpus Small Bones that form the Wrist
Carpals An alternative Name for the above
Deltoid A Muscle of the Arm
External-Communis-Digitorum A Muscle of the Forearm
Extensor-Carpii-Radialis-Longus As above
Flexor-Carpii-Ulnaris As above
Glenoid Cavity A Space in the Shoulder Blades to receive the Head of Humerus
Humerus A Bone of the Arm

Head Of Humerus A ball-shaped Knob at one end of the Humerus to articulate with the Scapula
Metacarpals Five Bones that form the back of the Hand
Metatarsals Five Bones of the Feet
Phalanges The Small Bones in the Fingers, Thumbs and Toes
Palmaris Longis A Muscle of the Forearm
Palmar Surface Appertaining to the Palm surface of the Hand
Radius A Bone of the Forearm
Supinator Radii Longus A Muscle of the Forearm
Triceps An Extensor Muscle of the Arm
Ulnar A Bone of the Forearm

ANATOMICAL REFERENCES OF THE LOWER EXTREMITIES

Acetabulum A Cavity in the Pelvis to receive the Head of Femur
Achilles Tendon A Tendon at the back of the Heel
Biceps Femoris Hamstring Muscle of the Thigh
Fibula A Bone of the Leg
Femur The Thigh Bone
Gastrocnemius The Calf Muscle
Ligamentum Patella A Ligament that keeps the Patella in position
Patella The Knee Cap
Popliteal Space The Space at the Back of the Knee
Plantar Arch The Arch underneath the Foot
Rectus Femoris An Extensor Muscle of the Thigh
Semimembranosus A Hamstring Muscle of the Thigh
Semitendinosus As above
Sartorius A Muscle of the Thigh
Sciatic Nerve Origin in the Buttocks, it Extends to the Thigh and the Leg
Tibia A Bone of the Leg
Vastus Externus, Medialis, Internus Extensor Muscles of the Thigh

Appendix

The following addresses supply equipment for the physical therapist including massage couches.

R. A. Dodd (Electro Medical) Ltd.,
12 Richmond Place,
Brighton,
Sussex.
BN2 2NA

John Bell and Croyden,
(Savory & Moore Ltd),
50–54 Wigmore Street,
London.
W1H 0AU.